Turning Curves

An Accountability Companion Reader

Mark Friedman

To order copies go to amazon.com
or resultsleadership.org

ISBN-13: 978-1519199355
ISBN-10: 151919935X

Parse Edition 2015
parsepublishing.org

Cover design: Justin Miklas
Interior design: Ross Feldner

To people
around the world
who are working to create
measurable improvements
for children, adults, families
and communities.

TABLE OF CONTENTS

CHAPTER 4: Choosing Performance Measures For Selected Services..69

CHAPTER 5: Putting Population and Performance Together (and stuff that didn't quite fit anywhere else) 82

CHAPTER 6: The Results Scorecard 94
by Marc Stone and Kayleigh Weaver

A Note about Notations: Throughout the book there are numerous references to pages in the book *Trying Hard Is Not Good Enough* (TH).Where pagination is different between the 2005 and 2015 editions, page references will be shown as (TH p. 135 / 140)

APPENDICES: 97

Notices regarding the free use of Results-Based Accountability™ (RBA) Outcomes-Based Accountability™ (OBA) material by government and nonprofit organizations: 158

Introduction

The story of Results-Based Accountability (RBA) begins on the African savannah more than two million years ago. Early hominids used elementary planning models to improve the performance of hunting and gathering. With the invention of agriculture about 10,000 years ago, these models proved inadequate. Life was more complicated, so planning models became more complicated. Since then the complexity of life has grown exponentially and planning models kept pace, so that by the end of the 20th Century planning had taken up all available work time. People were gathering data, sitting in meetings and writing reports for no good reasons at all. Precious time was wasted doing things that were simply not useful. A serious correction was needed. RBA emerged in the early 21st Century as one of the simplest planning models that humans could use to actually get things done. So whether you are hunting large game, sorting out the harvest, or running a government or nonprofit organization, RBA can help you get from talk to action without a lot of wasted effort.

RBA itself is presented in the book "Trying Hard Is Not Good Enough," (TH) and so will be explained only briefly here. Several entries near the beginning serve to review and reinforce the basic ideas. The main purpose of this book is to address questions about the implementation of RBA. Some of the topics are specific to RBA. Some are relevant to accountability in general. In each case, the intent is to start a conversation, not to provide definitive answers.

The overall organization of the book follows the structure of RBA itself: Population Accountability, Performance Accountability, and Putting Population and Performance Accountability together. An opening chapter addresses cross-cutting issues. There is a special section that addresses the selection of performance measures for some challenging types of service. Larger documents are presented in the appendices and should be viewed as integral to the book. That's basically it.

There is a lot of material here and you may not want to read it all. So I have asterisked the entries I really want you to read. These mostly appear near the beginning of each chapter. It wouldn't be a bad idea to read these first. Then you can decide if any of the other material warrants your attention.

Most of the entries are things I have written over the past 10 years, often in response to questions from the practitioner community. But the book includes several important essays written by others. I particularly want to thank (in order of appearance) Mark Funkhouser, Mike Pinnock, Nigel Richardson and Adam Hewitt, Ruth Jordan and Vicki Myson, Desiree Nangle, Marc Stone and Kayleigh Weaver for their contributions. David Burnby, Deitre Epps, Adam Luecking, Justin Miklas and Sharon Shea also made important contributions to the book. Thanks to Deanna Zachary for editing the book and to Justin Miklas for the cover design. And thanks to the many friends around the world who are using RBA, and whose work continues to be a source of learning and inspiration.

Finally, a note about names. The RBA framework is known in parts of the UK as Outcomes-Based Accountability (OBA), and, for this reason, I often refer to the framework with the acronym RBA/OBA. With a few exceptions, I will use just RBA for purposes of space and simplicity. You will sometimes see Results-Based Accountability™ and Outcomes Based Accountability™ referenced with the trademark symbol. This is to protect against those (thankfully) rare instances where these names are misused. It is not intended in any way to compromise or qualify the free use of RBA by government and nonprofit organizations. As a general rule, the trademark symbol needs to be used only once in a document, after which the names may be used without the symbol. Where use of the symbol is likely to be misinterpreted as restricting the free use of RBA, it may be omitted. Note that the acronyms RBA and OBA are **not** copyrighted and no trademark symbol should be used. RBA is also the acronym for the Royal Bank of Australia. OBA stands for the Ontario Beekeepers Association.

Chapter 1:
The RBA Framework As A Whole

*1. WHAT IS RBA?

This is an excerpt from Chapter 1 of "Trying Hard Is Not Good Enough." Chances are you have already read this, but it might not hurt to read it again. It might give you an idea about your elevator speech for RBA. When people (in an elevator) ask me what I do, I say "I help people work together to improve quality of life in their communities and improve the performance of their programs.[1]" It's not perfect. Twenty words. Maybe you can do better. The best elevator speech of all time belongs to the CEO of ICANN[2], the international organization that manages the internet. His speech: "We manage the dot in dot com." Impressive.

Results-Based Accountability (RBA), or Outcomes-Based Accountability (OBA) is a disciplined way of thinking and taking action that can be used to improve the quality of life in communities, cities, counties, states and nations. RBA can also be used to improve the performance of programs, agencies and service systems.

RBA starts with ends and works backward, step by step, to means. For communities, the ends are conditions of well-being for children, adults, families and the community as a whole such as *Children Ready for School, A Safe Neighborhood, A Clean and Sustainable Environment*, and *A Prosperous Inclusive Economy*. For programs, the ends are the ways customers are better off when the program works the way it should, such as the percent of people in a job training program who get and keep living wage jobs.

Many people have been frustrated by past efforts that were all talk and no action. RBA is a process that gets you and your partners from talk to action quickly. It uses plain language and common sense methods that everyone can understand. The most basic version of RBA can be done in less than an hour and produces ideas that can be acted on immediately. RBA is an inclusive process where diversity is an asset and everyone in the community can contribute. Like all meaningful processes, RBA is hard work. But it is work that that makes a difference in peoples' lives.

---

[1] For readers in the E.U., Australia and New Zealand, the term "program" will be used to mean "service."

[2] Internet Corporation for Assigned Names and Numbers

*2. MEASURING RESULTS IN THE REAL WORLD: A better way to link policy analysis and performance management

Mark Funkhouser, Publisher, *Governing Magazine*
March 2014, Reprinted with permission.

"Operation Breakthrough, a Kansas City social service agency founded in 1971 by two nuns, sits in one of the poorest parts of the city. It serves about 400 kids every day, 98 percent of whom come from families who live below the poverty line. About a quarter of the kids are homeless and another quarter are living in foster care.

Operation Breakthrough is one of dozens of nonprofits and government agencies trying to improve the lives of children and families in the city's urban core. It's clear that some of these agencies are doing vital work well. Yet Sister Berta Sailer says that conditions in the neighborhoods served have steadily worsened over the decades.

"How is it possible," asks Mark Friedman, "to have all these successful programs while conditions get worse?" This paradox forms the starting point for his 2005 book, *Trying Hard is Not Good Enough.* Friedman, who has more than 30 years of experience in public administration and public policy, has developed "results-based accountability," a system of performance improvement that is radically different from "logic models" and other more widely known approaches to policy analysis.

For most of my government career, I used logic models. When I came across Friedman's work, I was struck by the power and utility of results-based accountability. Logic models assume a linear relationship between actions and results that simply doesn't exist in the real world. And the strategies that policy analysts produce are often top-down. Friedman's approach is cleaner, simpler, more practical and less elitist. It's designed to answer three questions: How much are you doing? How well are you doing it? Is anyone better off? Think of it as policy analysis and performance management for populists.

The point of social service programs is to improve community conditions. But what about the fact that an individual program cannot do this? Friedman shows how to do "Population Accountability" at the city, county or state level and "Performance Accountability" at the program or agency level. Then he shows how to put the two together to demonstrate the linkage between population and customer results.

One strong convert to Friedman's system is Connecticut state Rep. Diana Urban. When Governing named her a Public Official of the Year in 2010, it called results-based accountability "the defining aspect" of her career. She says it lets legislators become a "functional part" of effective policymaking and cites a results-accountability review of the state's school-based health-care centers. The review documented that the highest use of the centers was for mental health issues and that the centers also were helping to reduce absenteeism by providing onsite health services. It showed that per-student cost was very low, resulting in funding for additional school health centers.

"The highest form of analysis is using intellect to aid interaction between people," the late public policy pioneer Aaron Wildavsky wrote more than three decades ago. Friedman's work shows in practical terms how language and common sense can be used to allow people to find common ground and improve their communities."

*3. COMPACTS AND CONVENTIONS

The physical world is made up of thousands of interlocking agreements about standard ways of doing things. My favorite example comes from the Franklin Institute in Philadelphia, where they have a display (similar to Figure 1) of all the different cross sections of railroad track that existed in the United States in the 19th century, before agreement on the current modern rail system. Before that, passengers and freight had to be loaded and unloaded at each terminus where different rail systems connected. Virtually every successful modern system, including the conventions underlying monetary and communication networks, has a similar set of agreements in place. Notice that agreeing on the size, shape and separation of the railroad rails leaves lots of room for innovation in the design of railroad cars, and does little to restrict the kinds of goods that can be transported.

There are some examples in social science too. National and state tax systems talk to each other. Many states have made progress on standardizing social benefit application forms across programs. But, generally, social systems lag far behind. Agreeing to use a core set of principles as the basis for an accountability compact, like the one developed in Vermont, is much like the railroad or computer agreement. It would not restrict content. It would simply give us a consistent way of working together.

Why should we use RBA as the basis for such an agreement? RBA has certain characteristics that make it uniquely suited for this purpose. RBA is the only planning model that provides a complete architecture for both Population and Performance Accountability, spanning the distance from broad quality of life conditions at the global and national levels to the performance of the smallest programs. RBA has the simplest set of core principles and language conventions that allow people using different systems to communicate with each other. RBA works across ALL government and nonprofit services, not just health, education, and social services. RBA can be cross-walked to any other framework; and any framework can be cross-walked to RBA. And RBA has an established track record of working across different organizational and social cultures. Using RBA core principles is precisely the kind of convention that is needed to move the government and nonprofit sectors past their 19th century railroad problem.

Figure 1.1

ADDENDUM: The following is an excerpt from Bill Bryson's book about Australia:

"The Indian Pacific is actually an infant as rail systems go, having been created as recently as 1969 when a new standard-gauge line was built across the country. Before that, for various arcane reasons mostly to do with regional distrust and envy, Australian railroad lines employed different gauges. New South Wales had rails 4 feet 8 1/2 inches apart. Victoria opted for a more commodious 5 feet 3 inches. Queensland and Western Australia economically decided on a standard of 3 feet 6 inches. South Australia, inventively, had all three. Five times on any journey between the east and west coasts, passengers and freight had to be off-loaded from one train and re-deposited on another." (*In a Sunburned Country*, Bill Bryson, 2000.)

*4. THE VERMONT ACCOUNTABILITY COMPACT AND ACT 186
(Appendix A & Appendix B)

The Vermont Accountability Compact (Appendix A) and Act 186 come from an historic agreement between the legislative branch, the executive branch, and the nonprofit community who came together in 2013 and 2014 with the conviction that common ways of thinking, talking and taking action together would make them more effective in working to improve the well-being of the people of Vermont.

The Compact was a precursor to Act 186 (Appendix B), which was signed by Governor Shumlin in June 2014. This legislation put many of the Compact's recommended RBA conventions into state law. Following on the groundbreaking work of Diana Urban in Connecticut, the Vermont law is now the most comprehensive legislation of its kind. Notable among the many who deserve credit for these accomplishments are: From the legislature, the bill's sponsors, Senator Diane Snelling (R) and Representative Anne O'Brien (D); From the executive branch, Agency of Human Services Secretary Doug Racine, Monica Hutt, Susan Bartlett and Drusilla Roessle; From the Governor's Office, Chief Performance Officer Sue Zeller; From the nonprofit sector, Anne Lezak, Lauren-Glenn Davitian, Scott Johnson, Kate Jellema, Martha Maksym, Eddie Gale..... and many others.

So, please, turn now to Appendix A and read the Compact. I know you don't want to do that right now. Appendices are almost always afterthoughts to be considered later if at all. But not so in the case of this book. I've put all the long documents at the back of the book so as not to disrupt the flow of the text. But the appendices here are as important as the main text. So please read the Vermont Compact. It will only take you two minutes. It's very impressive. You will be glad you did. And if you like the Compact, take a look at the legislation. Think about what version of these documents might make sense where you live. Thanks.

*5. THE SIMPLEST WAY TO IMPLEMENT RBA

If you're having trouble implementing RBA, try this approach:

POPULATION ACCOUNTABILITY:
>   Step 1: Pick an important population indicator.
>   Step 2: Run the Population Turn the Curve (TTC) Exercise. (TH Appendix E)[3]
>   Step 3: Take action.
>   Repeat.

PERFORMANCE ACCOUNTABILITY:
>   Step 1: Pick an important performance measure
>   Step 2: Run the Performance Turn the Curve Exercise. (TH Appendix E)
>   Step 3: Take action.
>   Repeat.

---

[3] We will use this convention to refer to parts of *Trying Hard Is Not Good Enough*. Both Turn the Curve exercises are also available from the Publications page of the FPSI website result-saccountability.com/publications.

The Turn the Curve exercises are the heart of RBA. In one hour, you can have the beginnings of an action plan and get started. RBA is a simple common sense set of methods, but there will always be ways of overcomplicating it. How often have we seen groups spend all their time "planning to plan to plan?" It can go on forever. If RBA is done right, it will be simple and useful. If it is not simple and useful, then chances are it's not being done right. Go back to these exercises and get back to the basics. Running a Turn the Curve exercise is also the BEST way to teach RBA to others. Skip the lecture, the video, the book and just try the exercise. People will get it. Then you can go back and teach the theory later.

*6. RBA AND NON-WESTERN CULTURES

The culture of any people is a precious possession to be preserved and protected. Different cultures have different world views and values that lead their societies to create unique and beautiful ways of living together. The question sometimes arises as to whether RBA, or any other planning framework, is a threat to social cultures. More specifically, is RBA a product of European/American culture that is potentially destructive to non-western cultures? My experience suggests not.

First and foremost the RBA framework is a set of tools, no different than any of the other tools of modern life like the telephone or computer. Tools take on meaning in how they are used. RBA can be used, like any tool, in ways that are meaningful to the culture using it.

RBA first allows the articulation of quality of life ambitions based on the values and the language of people using it. RBA has been used in at least ten different languages, including the languages of indigenous people.

Regarding the use of data, humans have been counting things since the earliest times of hunting, herding and harvesting. Use of numbers in one form or another belongs to all cultures. So too does the idea of numbers getting better or worse, the idea embedded in the RBA concept of a baseline.

Stories are the oldest way we capture, retain, and transmit knowledge in our societies. The step in RBA where we tell the story behind numbers draws on this ancient tradition. The idea of partnerships is equally old. And all cultures enable people to take action to make life better, the central purpose of RBA.

If RBA is a threat to any culture, then it is not being used properly. RBA used properly adapts to and is respectful of all cultures.

There is much more to say on this subject. I encourage others to offer their experience and perspective.

Thanks to Sharon Shea for the following comment. Sharon Shea is one of the leading RBA experts in New Zealand: *Tena Koutou (Greetings to All). Speaking as an Indigenous RBA consultant based in New Zealand, I can confirm Mark's comments and add that all of my Indigenous clients are using RBA as a tool to articulate their cultural interpretation of population and performance outcomes. The integrity of the tool lies in its application and ensuring that cultural context is respected and prioritised at all times. Nga mihi*, Sharon Shea.

*7. SOME REFLECTIONS ON HOW TO KEEP RBA FLEXIBLE AND USEFUL WHILE MAINTAINING ITS INTELLECTUAL INTEGRITY.

I have tried to make RBA into a set of ideas that are adaptable to new situations, not a rigid ideology that must be implemented in a particular way. This is partly a matter of philosophy and partly a matter of practicality. Only adaptive systems succeed. Rigid systems are doomed to fail.

This then creates a dilemma for which I do not have a perfect answer. How much can you change RBA and still have it be RBA? This is a surprisingly difficult question to answer. The traditional rigid answer falls back on copyright protection. "All ideas must be attributed, and change is prohibited." This is the rigid doomed-to-fail approach and so must be rejected. But where then to draw the line on what is and isn't RBA?

First and foremost, it is important to recognize that **RBA is a container**. All planning and management models are containers. They hold the content that people put into them. If we define a "population result" as a "condition of well-being for children, adults, families and communities," then there are no "right" or "wrong" population results. "All children are healthy" is a population result, as is "All people have toothbrushes." The content of a population result is up to the user of the model. It is the same with all other components of RBA. So the line drawing about what is or is not RBA has nothing to do with content.

But if you were to tinker with the structure of the model itself, then the tinkered version becomes less RBA and more of something else. With enough tinkering over time, RBA could become unrecognizable. And this is a problem for two reasons. The first reason is that the tinkering may not be an improvement and may even have significant negative effects. There is a deep principle in evolutionary biology that says that the great majority of mutations are harmful. RBA is a carefully constructed whole. The parts are all interconnected in important ways, something like a living organism. If you make one part of RBA less functional, then the whole might not function so well. It will then be less helpful to the people who need help.

The second problem has to do with the ways in which ideas spread through groups, countries and civilizations (See the essay below on the diffusion of innovations). Some ideas are simple and powerful. When the wheel was first introduced, other ways to use it became immediately obvious. The recent evidence for this is the explosive growth in the use of wheeled luggage, which by some accounts, is the fastest diffusion of innovation on record. But how do more complex ideas diffuse while still maintaining their integrity? That is the problem. And the answer has something to do with "branding" and consistency of message. Partly for this reason, we have begun to use the trademark symbol for Results-Based Accountability™ (RBA) & Outcomes-Based Accountability™ (OBA). The RBA and OBA brand is becoming well known, and has grown amazingly fast around the world. But the brand needs to stand for something. It can not be just any version of RBA. The "official" version of RBA is, of course, in the book "Trying Hard Is Not Good Enough." The book and DVD are the primary tools for quality control. But what if people implement and teach RBA in ways that differ from the book? The reputation of the brand could be damaged and this could slow the spread of the ideas. This actually happened in NSW Australia a few years ago and we are still dealing with the consequences.

Then there is the matter of control. Once you put an idea out in the world you lose control over how it is used. Copyrights and trademarks give some protection. But for all practical purposes, someone in my situation must simply "get over" the idea that you can control how RBA is understood and used. So whatever we do to preserve the intellectual integrity of the model must be done through persuasion and not force. (If you want to see how this is done through force, look at any community change model that franchises its work.) There are moral problems with restricting the use of social innovations, which is why RBA is, and always will be, free for use by government and nonprofit organizations.

So that takes us back to the "line drawing" question. I need to persuade people that there are certain parts of RBA that shouldn't be tampered with because such tampering compromises the model and makes it less useful. And because creating a less useful model that is STILL CALLED RBA undermines the "brand" and makes it less likely that RBA will grow and prosper.

Whew!

So what are the core elements that people should not tamper with? Here is another dilemma. Any author will tell you that his or her words and ideas are like their children and they can not let go of any of them. This is why most books never get finished and many that do get finished are badly written. Authors often can't do their own editing or endure the editing of others. I am no different. All the ideas in RBA are important to me and I don't want to let go of any of them. Of course, I did just that in writing "Trying Hard Is Not Good Enough." There is much that was edited out. And every time I do a workshop, I must select the slides I have time to show and those which must be set aside. Furthermore, I preach that people should pick 3 to 5 measures and get on with it. So, there is a certain "practice what you preach" thing going on here.

Back to drawing the line. Years ago, I was asked to come up with a simple way for people to remember what is different about RBA and we developed the 2-3-7 pneumonic. RBA has **two** different kinds of accountability, **three** different types of performance measures and **seven** questions that can get you from talk to action in about an hour. Inside these three elements are 10 ideas, shown in **bold** below, that represent the core of RBA that I think should be preserved.[4]

2 KINDS OF ACCOUNTABILITY PLUS LANGUAGE DISCIPLINE

The distinction between (1) **Population Accountability** and (2) **Performance Accountability** is the single most important idea in RBA. Keeping these separate yet connected is the only way to do either one well.

It is necessary to adopt a language discipline to support this distinction, hence the definitions within Population Accountability of (3) **Population Results** and (4) **Indicators**. Population results are quality of life conditions (or aspirations) for people in a geographic area. Indicators tell the extent to which these conditions are being achieved. Within Performance Accountability, (5) **Performance measures** serve as a class of measures that tell if a program, agency or service system is working.

3 KINDS OF PERFORMANCE MEASURES
(6) *How much did we do?*
(7) *How well did we do it?*
(8) *Is anyone better off?*

This categorization scheme for performance measures is a significant innovation that replaces the mountain of jargon we have struggled with for decades. It makes performance measurement into something that is understandable to managers and stakeholders. "Is anyone better off?" is the voice of the taxpayer and everyday citizen. It is the reason we do this work.

---

[4] Remember that words are just labels for ideas. These are the 10 labels I most often use, understanding that other labels have been chosen in other places and other languages.

7 QUESTIONS FROM ENDS TO MEANS IN LESS THAN AN HOUR

(9) **Baselines** and
(10) **Turning the curve**

Baselines, with history and forecast, show where we have been and where we're headed. Are things getting better or worse? The story behind the baseline opens up an inclusive conversation about causes. The word "story" is important because it is the oldest way we communicate and opens the process to non-experts. This is a more sophisticated and fair way to track progress, particularly in complex change processes.

The two different versions of the 7 Questions get you from talk to action at both the population and performance levels. They form the basis for the Turn the Curve exercises that can get any group to the beginnings of an action plan in less than an hour. The Turn the Curve report format can be used to structure understandable processes and documents. And they can produce real change in peoples' lives when used properly.

Now, for some reason, most people are willing to go with the 2 kinds of accountability and 3 kinds of performance measures without changing anything. But everyone seems to want to come up with their own version of the population and performance 7 questions. Why is that? I think it's because people see the intention of the seven questions and think they can do better. "Hell, it's just common sense. If we put it in our own words, then we can adapt it to the audience we are working with and they will understand it better and it will be more useful." I get this. It is not really a bad line of reasoning.

But here's the problem: The 7 questions, like everything else in RBA, are very carefully thought out. There are reasons behind every word. So how much paraphrasing is OK? And that brings us to our last (for now) dilemma: the difference between TEACHING RBA and USING RBA. Tinkering with the wording of the 7 questions might be OK in USING RBA, but may NOT be OK in TEACHING RBA. Imagine if you were taking a class in constitutional law, and the teacher said, "We're not going to be using the actual constitution in this class, but a version that I like better." You would immediately see the problem. Nothing wrong with the professor explaining why he likes his version of the constitution better. But the original is still there as a starting point. I am not saying that RBA is like the US Constitution, but you get the idea. If RBA is taught using only interpretations, without the original, then the original is effectively lost.

I have tried to get people to do this, to teach at least the core concepts of RBA faithfully. Then when using RBA, show the 7 questions exactly as they appear in the book and clearly distinguish any interpretations or additions (e.g. by putting them in parentheses). Then we can all be clear which are the original ideas and which are the adaptations. Surely this is reasonable, don't you think? But it's damn difficult (and time consuming) to keep dealing with this. I am not, and never will be, the RBA police. I go back and forth between wanting to make this work and giving up. Here I am trying to make it work again. If it doesn't work this time, I may give up........no, not really.........

*8. IF IT'S NOT USEFUL DON'T DO IT.

(Almost the title of this book[5])

I don't dislike double negatives. Think of the alternative, "If it's useful, do it." Meaningless. Anyone who works in an organization whether government, nonprofit or for-profit is familiar with the idea of useless process. It requires no definition, but let's try just for fun. Useless process is work that does not advance the purposes of the organization. It does not contribute to making the agency work better (*How well did we do it?*) and it does not contribute to customer outcomes (*Is anyone better off?*).

There are three ways in which organizations commonly waste time, and RBA provides methods for addressing each.

- **Collecting data we don't use**: RBA provides concrete methods to identify the most important measures and use them to improve performance.

- **Meetings that go on too long and don't produce anything**: RBA provides a meeting agenda that mirrors the Turn the Curve[6] thinking process and allows groups to continuously improve action plans.

- **Reports that are too long, too complicated and not used**: RBA provides simple but powerful report formats that can be used for reporting on population quality of life and for performance reporting, budgeting and planning.

---

[5] Also almost the title of the book was my wife Terry Wilson's suggestion: *Sex, Lies and Accountability*.

[6] I have been thinking of adding the ™ symbol to the phrase "Turn the Curve" or "Turning the Curve." These phrases are RBA inventions and the RBA framework itself is known as Turning the Curve in some parts of the world. But adding another trademark symbol to the use of RBA seems like an un-necessary intrusion. So I have decided for now not to do this, at least until there is some evidence of misuse. The Turn the Curve thinking process is also known as The Leaking Roof thinking process. (See TH p. 28)

So why do we do this? We are smart committed people. We believe in the work that we're doing. Where did useless process come from and why do we put up with it?

Let's take "where did it come from" first. Whenever you have two or more people, you have differences of opinion about how things should be done. As people move in and out of power, and as laws change, new processes are put in place and old processes are redefined. Once a process is put in place, it takes considerable effort to change it, and even more effort to get rid of it altogether. House-cleanings come rarely. Processes develop adherents. Sometimes this is legitimate support for an important part of the organization's work. More often it is "because we have always done it this way."

Now why do we put up with it? For every bit of useless process there is a history associated with its establishment and a sacred list of reasons for its continuance. People come to accept the process as normal. We don't even think of changing or abandoning such processes. They are passively accepted without question as something either out of the organization's control or too difficult to change. RBA provides a template against which to test current processes. If the corresponding RBA process is simpler and more effective than the current process, you can make a case for change.

Here's a trick guaranteed to simplify your work over time. Make all plans and reports no more than one or two pages. Put all additional detail you think might be needed into appendices. As in dialectical processes, the appendices will wither away over time. What else could we stop doing that would create more time for useful work? Apply the RBA criteria: Simple, common sense, plain language, minimum paper, useful. If something doesn't meet this test then fix it or get rid of it. Make a list. Do it.

Now here's an important thing to remember. Please don't allow RBA to create useless work. If you can't think of 3 to 5 measures, then use one or two. If a particular unit is not ready to use RBA, move on to working with the one that is ready. If RBA reporting becomes a burden, cut it back, make it less frequent or eliminate it. In other words, RBA itself, in whole or in part, can and must be sacrificed if its effect, for whatever reason, is the creation of useless work.

*9. *HOW OUTCOMES SAVED MY LIFE (OR AT LEAST MY SANITY*
by Mike Pinnock (Appendix C)

The November 2012 issue of the New Zealand journal *Social Work Now* published this terrific article by Mike Pinnock. Mike was one of the first people in the UK to recognize the value of RBA and begin using it. Mike has made tremendous contributions to the development and use of OBA across the UK. In this article, he makes a compelling case for the importance of both population and performance outcomes. He is a great story teller and you'll enjoy both the style and substance of the article. Thanks to the New Zealand Ministry for Social Development for permission to reprint it here.

*10. *TRANSFORMING LIFE CHANCES FOR CHILDREN, YOUNG PEOPLE AND FAMILIES IN LEEDS, UK USING OUTCOMES-BASED ACCOUNTABILITY*
by Nigel Richardson and Adam Hewitt (Appendix D)

Leeds is the third largest city in the UK. This is the inspiring story of how the city moved from failing services for children and young people in 2010 to the highest rated local authority in the country in 2015. There are lessons here about the use of OBA, about turned curves and changed culture, but most importantly about the crucial role of strong leadership.

*11. THE IMPORTANCE OF PARALLEL IMPLEMENTATION WITHIN RBA

As a general rule you should always think of RBA implementation as running on a set of parallel tracks. Most importantly, population work does not have to be done before performance work can begin. They can and should be done in parallel. Within each track many activities will also run in parallel.

At the population level, there will be a track for identifying population results and indicators, gathering the data, and creating reports on quality of life. While this is happening, you also want people to get started on turning curves as soon as possible. You should run training sessions, including the Turn the Curve exercises, as often and widely as possible. And consider starting a for-real non-exercise Turn the Curve process. The Data Development Agenda will also proceed in parallel with this, as will the Information and Research Agenda.

At the performance level, work should proceed from both the bottom up and the top down. At the "bottom" of the organization, the level of individual programs and services, you should use the TH Appendix G 5-step process to identify performance measures (headline, secondary and data development) for each program ONE AT A TIME. Stage this over time, starting with just 2 or 3 programs. The measures identified in this step can then be used at higher levels in the organization. (See "Building a Performance Foundation in your organization" below.)

At the "top" begin by posting indicator baselines on the wall of the conference room. These should be the most important population indicators to which the organization contributes. You do not have to wait for the larger more inclusive political process of selecting population results and indicators. You can identify results and indicators as a working set to use while you advocate for, or participate in, the larger process.

You can start performance measurement work even in the absence of any serious population work. This is usually what happens. Performance measures should be used as soon as possible in management, budgeting, and strategic planning. The Next Generation Contracting agenda (Appendix I) can be used to bring RBA concepts to contracting. And people should take turns presenting program performance in Turn the Curve format at staff meetings. At all levels, people should begin to use the Performance Accountability 7 Questions in supervisory meetings. These should lead to a stable "routine" process of continuous improvement. And there should be performance measures on the walls across the agency.

The RBA Implementation Self Assessment Questionnaire (SAQ) (Appendix G) can be viewed as an implementation check-list. Review this carefully and see what you've already done, where you can get started quickly and what pieces need to be staged over a longer period. Use the SAQ to compute an implementation score and create a baseline. Think about turning the curve on the SAQ score. Use the SAQ to understand the details of parallel implementation of RBA.

*12. THE DIFFUSION OF INNOVATION: WHAT THE RESEARCH TELLS US ABOUT THE HISTORY (AND POTENTIAL) GROWTH OF RBA?

I strongly encourage anyone involved in spreading the word about RBA (or any other new ideas) to read "Diffusion of Innovations" by Everett M. Rogers (2003). Thanks to Gail Hayes for bringing this book to my attention. It is easy to read, fascinating and useful.

Rogers defines diffusion of innovation (p. 11) as:
> *... a process by which*
> *(1) an innovation*
> *(2) is communicated through certain channels*
> *(3) over time*
> *(4) among the members of a social system.*

He then presents five stages in the acceptance or rejection of an innovation by an individual or organization *(p. 20)*:
> *(1) knowledge,*
> *(2) persuasion,*
> *(3) decision,*
> *(4) implementation, and*
> *(5) confirmation*

Here are, what seem to me, some immediate lessons for our work:

1. **Understanding RBA configuration and extent of use**: We think of RBA as a single innovation, but it is, in fact, a collection of interrelated innovations that can sometimes be adopted in different configurations. For example, an organization (e.g. community partnership) might work on Population Accountability but not Performance Accountability. Similarly, an organization (e.g. a school) might work on Performance Accountability and not Population Accountability.

Within each of these areas, there are further component innovations. One is the Turn the Curve (TTC) thinking process which operates in both the population and performance levels. This innovation may be taken as a whole (and we hope it is). But there are then innovations within this innovation which are arguably separable,[7] including the use of "baselines" with forecast(s), the emphasis on "no-cost / low-cost" and "crazy" ideas, the idea of a Data Development Agenda, and Information and Research Agenda.

The Turn the Curve exercise can even be used without any data, under certain circumstances. The data stage can be replaced (wholly or partially) with estimated data or with a simple coding system indicating the current state of a measure (OK, not OK) and trend direction (getting better, worse or about the same). While we might hope that people "completely" adopt RBA, and completely adopt the Turn the Curve process, this does not always happen in actual practice.

The concept of "partners" is certainly not new, but there is a deeper type of consideration of potential partners within the TTC discussion because of the more immediate focus on action. The idea of getting from "Talk to Action" in one hour is arguably a kind of innovation. Within Performance Accountability there are the three "innovative" performance measurement categories that replace historical jargon with *How much did we do? How well did we do it? Is anyone better off?*.

This mix and match approach to RBA implementation is not without its problems. It is potentially fragmented and could leave out important components and connections. But the complete implementation of RBA is an ideal that will only rarely be achieved.

If RBA component innovations are separable, what does this mean for our approach to teaching the ideas and promoting/supporting implementation? First, I think it means we must not be too fixated on the notion of complete implementation of RBA. Instead we must think in terms of helping people and organizations adopt the configuration of RBA components best suited to their needs.

---

[7] By separable I mean, the overall innovation can be adopted with some elements omitted or revised. This is the stage Rogers calls "re-invention."

This also means, ironically, that we have a difficult time quantifying the extent of RBA use. If no two places are implementing RBA exactly the same way, at what point can we say that a given organization or jurisdiction is "using RBA." There are many possible meanings for this phrase. We currently estimate usage with number/percentage of US states and number/percentage of countries where RBA "has been used." Within these categories we have some additional detail about specific groups and organizations. But it is certain that the user community is much larger than the groups we work with directly. For example, we know that there are a certain number of state and county health departments in the US using RBA to structure their jurisdiction's health plan and oversee the area health system. But RBA has been discussed in many different health forums, and it is likely that there are state and county health departments using RBA that we don't know about. We also know of some places where RBA was used at one point in time but may not be used now. It is not clear how one would go about answering the question of extent of use. It would be complex research in the health system alone.

Here's what we think we know now. RBA has been used in 15 to 20 countries. We know that RBA has been taught and used in more than 40 of the US states. We know the total number of books sold (more than 48,000 at the time of this writing), but have very limited information on where these book orders come from. We know the exact extent of worldwide use of the Results Scorecard (See Chapter 6). It's time we moved to develop more refined "usage" metrics, and encourage RBA advocates to do the same for their jurisdictions.

2. **Systematically using communication channels**: Innovations may be adopted by individuals, organizations and systems of organizations. We work with organizations at the national, regional, state, council/county, city, and neighborhood levels. We work with organizations that do everything from child care to transportation to national security.

At any given time we are actively involved, in many US states and many countries, all with their own corresponding complex network of social and political systems. And there are meta-systems, such as global networks that develop physically in conferences and virtually from professional associations and contact on the internet.

This is a much more complex diffusion challenge than a for-profit company selling a product in a defined market. These facts, first, require a certain agility. We need to know something about all the different programs and cultural settings of potential RBA adopters. Working with a department of transportation in the US is very different from working with a Safeguarding Children Board in the UK or a Whanau Ora Collective in New Zealand. This means we must be humble and willing to learn. No one comes to this work with anywhere near the necessary breadth of knowledge and experience. It also means that we could perhaps be more intentional in the way we approach different networks. RBA growth has been mostly opportunistic. We have followed the interests and connections as they have developed. This may be the best way to continue. But, maybe we should think about placing greater emphasis on reaching particular groups in particular places?

3. **Meeting people where they are**: And we must begin to think more analytically about where people are in the adoption process *"(1) knowledge, (2) persuasion, (3) decision, (4) implementation, and (5) confirmation."* Think about any of the conferences or conference workshops that have been devoted to RBA. There are people in the audience at all different stages of the adoption process. All the people who come have at least heard about RBA and therefore have some "knowledge" of RBA. Some may already be persuaded to try it. A few may have decided to use RBA and are actually using it. I think it is safe to say that the large majority of attendees are at the persuasion stage. They have heard about RBA. They want to know what it is, how it works and, most importantly, how it could help them in their particular circumstances. This is the information gathering that Rogers talks about as essential to the diffusion process.

If this depiction of the audience is true, then we should deliberately address these questions in the structure of our workshops and our use of other communication channels. We need to tell potential adopters (1) What RBA is, (2) How it works and (3) How it could help them. We need to communicate the extent to which others like them have used RBA successfully.

And we need to anticipate that the next stage, the "decision" stage to use or not use RBA, will depend in part on how complex and difficult it appears to be. One of RBA's virtues is its simplicity of structure, its use of plain language, and the relative ease with which parts can be adopted quickly. Many people in RBA workshops have gone back from the workshop and used the Turn the Curve exercise or the three performance measurement questions immediately.

But we know that deeper implementation of RBA, up to and including organizational culture change, is not easy. There are many ways in which this kind of change can stall or go astray. We have lists of "pitfalls" and "lessons learned. But these kinds of warnings are not necessarily helpful to those in the early stages of considering RBA. There is a danger that this information could work against RBA at the "persuasion stage" of diffusion, as people ponder how it could help them or not. If RBA sounds too hard and risky, if we are not thoughtful about how we describe benefits vs. challenges, we could jeopardize the single most important part of teaching RBA, or any other set of ideas: the willingness of listeners to "give it a try."

*13. IF YOU COULD MAKE ONE NUMBER BETTER IN THE NEXT THREE YEARS, WHAT WOULD IT BE? (Also: If this program works well, what number gets better?)

People who try to do everything at once usually make little or no progress on anything. It is important to start somewhere. Pick a curve to turn and get started. As Con Hogan says "Anywhere leads to everywhere." But which curve?

In community work, there will be a constituency for every curve advocating that their curve should be the first one to be worked on. In this situation, I have found that there is a powerful question that can quickly create consensus about where to start. "If you could make one number better in the next three years, what would it be?" Groups can often quickly identify a curve they all want to turn. In some cases there are two or even three curves identified. And that's OK. Set up one (two or three) Turn the Curve tables, assemble the co-conspirators, and get started.

I have used a variation of this question in two places in my RBA lectures. At the end of the Population Accountability part of RBA, when I have presented the examples of where people have succeeded in turning a population indicator curve, I ask, "So what kind of story like this do you want to be able to tell about your (city, county, state or nation) in the next two or three years?" If this question works, people are quiet for a minute. Some people might start thinking, "We can do this. And I know where I want to start." If you allow time for discussion of next steps, a ball might start rolling.

I ask the same question at the end of the Performance segment, after we have looked at examples of where people have succeeded in turning an important performance measure curve. Although for Performance Accountability, the period needs to be shortened. If you could turn one curve in the next 6 to 12 months what would it be?

There is a variation on this question that is quite powerful for program performance. "If your program/service is wildly successful, what number gets better?" This question can often move the conversation directly to the most powerful *Better Off?* measure and energizes the whole notion of measuring and improving performance. This can also be used when presented with a strategy devoid of measurement (a surprisingly common occurrence in government documents). If this strategy works well, what number gets better?

Try this next time you are working with a group. See if it gets people to move from the theory of RBA to an intention to actually turn a curve.

14. TOOL FOR CHOOSING A COMMON LANGUAGE (Appendix E)

The Tool for Choosing a Common Language (TCCL) has two purposes. First, I use it as a teaching tool in the two-day Training for Trainers and Coaches. Each group of four is given 20 minutes to identify the words their group would choose for each idea. Choosing language is a new experience for most people and this reinforces the notion that words are just labels for ideas. It's not the labels that matter but the ideas.

This exercise is intended to change the prevailing view that words have fixed meanings. Labels are important only because they provide a useful shorthand for talking about ideas. This provides people trained in RBA with an intellectual dexterity not easily gained from other methods. Once you know how to use words to label RBA ideas, you can sit in a meeting and figure out what people are talking about no matter what words they use. And perhaps you can help them move toward greater discipline in language usage.

The second purpose is to help organizations that want to adopt a standard language convention as part of RBA implementation. In this case, a small committee should be formed to consider the choices and come back to the executive team with a set of recommendations. These definitions can then be shared throughout the organization. It is not a bad idea to put the definitions of the top 10 RBA ideas on a poster that can be placed in conference rooms. Another poster (or two) could include the 7 Population and Performance Accountability questions. All of that in addition to the population and performance baseline curves you are trying to turn.

It is very important to understand that completing the TCCL is NOT intended for RBA beginners. I show people the TCCL in RBA 101 as a way of explaining the idea of language choice. But, when you teach RBA, do NOT run this as an exercise in an introductory class. In the early stages of learning about RBA, beginners can be confused by too many choices. You can use the TCCL to make sure your own language usage is clear and consistent.

15. THE IMPORTANCE OF FORECASTS:

Forecasts shift the conversation into the future. The usual state of affairs with government and non-profit data, and social data in general, is that the most recent data is not very recent. This often discourages people from using data at all. After all, what is the point of talking about the teen pregnancy rate from three years ago or even one year ago? Forecasting can be a powerful tool for shifting the data discussion from the past into the future.

When creating a forecast, you must first bring the data up to the present using the group's collective knowledge about what has happened in the intervening period. And, going forward, you must judge what will happen if you don't do something more or different than what you are doing now.[8] This discussion of "Where are we headed?" or "OMG. Look where we'll be in a few years unless we do something!" can help shape a feeling of common purpose and provide a sense of urgency about the need for action. Suddenly data is not about ancient history but about the very real present and the very likely future, and about our need to work together if we want that future to be different.

Forecasts, of course, also allow you to define success as "turning the curve" and can later be used to quantify the value of progress when a curve has actually turned. This is particularly important when progress consists of slowing, but not reversing, a bad trend.

Forecasts are not always needed. The trend direction might be obvious and a formal forecast might be a distraction. Sometimes just leaving room for an out-year forecast is enough to call the question and get the benefits of forecasting without actually presenting one. Use your judgment. But I see a lot of graphs with nothing but old historical data. And when that happens, the discussion of possible futures often gives way to complaining about the past.

16. SOME THOUGHTS ON FUNDING ONLY EVIDENCE-BASED PRACTICE

"The Mothers Against Drunk Driving (MADD) story teaches us not to wait for a federal grant, not to wait for the research community to give us the proven answer, and not to measure our success by how many projects we have implemented or how much money we have raised, but by whether the curve has turned." (TH p. 16)

"Research is important, but it is also important that the thinking of the group not be limited by the research. The research world can only tell us a fraction of what we need to know. We've got to make sure we use our own common sense, our own life experience, and our own knowledge of the communities in which we live. Something that has worked somewhere else might not work so well in your community. There must be room for learning and innovation." (TH pp. 42-43)

Funding only evidence-based programs not only limits our access to new ideas, but it can have the unintended consequence of discouraging involvement of the community

---

[8] Note, the correct phrasing of this question is NOT "What is the forecast if we do nothing?" Nothing is not an option. You must take into account things that are currently being done and things that are certain to happen. The correct phrasing is therefore "What is the forecast if we don't do anything more or different from/than what we are doing now?"

in deciding *what works*. If governments use their funds only for research proven practice, then the group of people who participate in the discussion of what can and should be done is effectively reduced to the academic community that produces the evidence. This actually lessens the chance of success by failing to tap the energy and innovation that comes from communities working together to turn curves. Evidence-based practice warrants due respect and consideration, but it can't be the only thing we fund.

In the next essay we take note of groundbreaking papers that argue for a broader approach to what counts as evidence.

17. Review: *EXPANDING THE EVIDENCE UNIVERSE: DOING BETTER BY KNOWING MORE*[9] by Lisbeth Schorr and Frank Farrow

In this paper published by the Center for the Study of Social Policy, authors Lisbeth Schorr and Frank Farrow argue for a much broader conception of evidence considered allowable in funding decisions by government and philanthropic agencies. The legitimate interest in funding evidence-based practice has led to an over-reliance on Random Control Trials (RCT) as the only legitimate source of knowledge about *what works*. This has limited our vision of what programs and strategies should be funded and diminished our chances of making a difference at scale on outcomes for children, families, and communities. As stated by the authors, "We must agree that the value of many kinds of interventions can be assessed, weighed, understood, and acted upon without having to be proven through experimental methods." The paper goes on to present specific recommendations for changes in policy and practice for funders and for the research and evaluation community. The paper also urges use of results-based planning and decision-making processes (e.g. RBA), as central components of community change and system change initiatives, to generate "real time" data, learning and accountability.

This is possibly the only scholarly paper to date to challenge the prevailing "wisdom" that we should fund ONLY research-proven programs and practice. The overly cautious research-proven policy is driven by the sensible notion that, if money is scarce, we should fund programs with the best chance of success. If a program has been proven by research, it has a better chance of working than a program that has not been tested.

The problem is that this greatly limits the ideas that can be considered and creates too small a playing field on which to attack our society's most serious problems. Not all

---

[9] cssp.org/publications/harold-richman-public-policy-symposium/Expanding-Evidence-the-Evidence-Universe_Doing-Better-by-Knowing-More_December-2011.pdf and the updated paper by Lisbeth Schorr, Frank Farrow and Joshua Sparrow (Friends of Evidence) at cssp.org/policy/evidence/AN-EVIDENCE-FRAMEWORK-TO-IMPROVE-RESULTS.pdf

good ideas have been tested by research or ever will be. Few if any *no-cost/low-cost* ideas have been formally studied. And research studies rarely test the kind of complex combinations of efforts necessary to turn population indicator curves.

This paper sets out a more practical and realistic way of looking at the question of evidence and the question of *what works*. If the paper reaches its intended audience, it will cause government and non-government funders to reconsider their overly cautious policies on evidence. It will also allow us to make funding decisions based on the best available knowledge of what works, even if this knowledge does not always meet narrow RCT standards.

While I am appreciative of the paper's support for RBA, it does not make reference to the evidentiary standard for demonstrating contribution to community change proposed in TH Chapter 7 (pp. 131-133/ 136 - 139). This standard imposes four tests on a claim for contribution: 1) There was a serious effort at sufficient scale to plausibly affect a population indicator or performance measure baseline; 2) There was a timely relationship to 3) a turn in the curve, and; 4) A relevant background trend stayed the same or got worse. This approach to evidence is the only way to show the effectiveness of complex community-based efforts like Promise Neighborhoods. It is essential that funders move to recognize and endorse this approach to evidence.

18. USING DATA FOR IMPROVEMENT NOT PUNISHMENT

We all have experience with numbers being used to pass summary judgment on our success or failure. From tests in school to budgets at work, we have become accustomed to thinking that the very purpose of numbers is to pass judgment. But one of my hopes for RBA is that it helps to fight this ingrained view. The first purpose of numbers, in my opinion, is not to pass judgment, but rather to figure out how to do better.

The attitude of management is of the upmost importance. The message has to be "Let's figure out what's going on here and what we can do together." RBA provides a structure for this discussion. The *Story behind the curve* is crucial. We need to invest the time necessary to understand what is going on behind the numbers. This can not be a cursory assessment. It means getting into the specifics of individual cases where things did not work out, asking what could have been done better in that particular case, and then looking across cases for patterns. It means developing a deep understanding of the community forces affecting our work that we do not control. It means looking for opportunities to work differently with partners.

This is not a postmortem on "why we failed" but rather a pro-active study of what can be done in the future. People naturally feel better if they are on offense, rather than defense. We then need the patience to watch to see if the changes we make are having the desired effect. And then go back through the learning process again on a regular basis. If nothing else, at least reward people for taking this process seriously. My favorite reward is pizza. People will do anything for pizza.

Sometimes bad numbers will drive some people to think that measurement itself is not worth it. I understand that feeling. But if life teaches you anything, it is to get up when you're knocked down. When bad numbers get you down, get up and work to fix them.

It is rarely the case that everything looks bad. There will always be accomplishments to celebrate and stories to tell about the people whose lives we helped for the better.

19. WHY THE TURN THE CURVE EXERCISES USE SELF-MANAGED GROUPS

The Turn the Curve exercises are designed for groups that are "self managed," and it almost always works well that way. This arrangement forces people to take ownership of the process. There is no expert they can defer to. And the experiential learning which comes from this exercise is the most powerful and important part of RBA 101.

One RBA consultant expressed concern that the groups sometimes get off topic without a facilitator. It might be worth creating another role for a group member in addition to the timekeeper and reporter roles. The third role could be that of "Topic Keeper."

There are two dangers that go with adding a facilitator. First, facilitation is difficult to do well and it's hard to find people with the skills to staff each table in a large group. It places a very big obstacle in the way of using the exercise if you always have to have expert facilitation in each group. Second, it is all too easy for the facilitator to take on a role of authority that checks the natural energy and enthusiasm that comes with the exercise.

You can also address this problem by going from group to group, listening in and helping them get unstuck if they get off topic. I always check in with groups about 10 minutes into the exercise to make sure they have a baseline with a forecast. If they get stuck anywhere it is usually here. The question I ask is "Who has the baseline with the official forecast?" Often people will have the history but not the forecast. Or they will have drawn the forecast to show where they **want** to go, not where they **are going**. Sometimes, they have discussed both history and forecast but haven't actually drawn it. The visual here is very important, so I gently insist that they draw it out. If they get the baseline right, the rest of the exercise usually goes well.

The second common mistake comes when groups are writing up the final one page report in the population exercise. The top of that report should show a population result like "Healthy People," but it is not uncommon for people to write something like "Decrease the obesity rate." This is not a population result but a change statement about an indicator. In this case you have to help them get a legitimate population result, e.g. Healthy People, at the top of the page and show them that the "Obesity Rate" is the title of the baseline graph.

20. OVER-PROMISING

One way to explain the importance of RBA to elected officials makes use of the idea of overpromising. Elected officials know a lot about overpromising, because promises not kept are talking points for their opponents in the next election.

If you understand the idea of Population Accountability, you know that the challenge of improving quality of life is bigger than programs and agencies, and bigger than government itself. So when an elected leader promises that the government BY ITSELF will "deliver" quality of life improvements or turn the curve on an important population indicator, it is always overpromising. Population curves can only be turned through partnerships, where government can lead, but not "deliver."[10]

Population Accountability gives elected officials a different conceptual model and different vocabulary to talk about quality of life ambitions without overpromising. "We all want a safe community." "Here's what the data tell us." "Here's how WE can work together to make this change."

There are parallels to this in talking with senior managers in government and non-profit agencies about turning performance curves as well. "What's the *story behind the curve*?" "Who are the partners that can help us?" "How can we, the management, staff and partners, work together to make this change?"

Have you seen examples of overpromising? Do you think this issue can be an effective way to open a conversation about using RBA?

21. The BOOK CLUB (AND CURRICULUM) APPROACH

Okay let's face it. Reading a book is not always an easy thing to do. Many of us put off reading books. But here's an easy way to read "Trying Hard is Not Good Enough." Consider reading it as a group as if you were in a book club.

---

[10] The phrase "delivering outcomes" is problematic for this reason.

This is how you could divide the chapters into segments that could be addressed in a series of nine book club meetings (or university classes). If you met once a week, it would take about two months.

Session 1: Prologue, Introduction and Chapter 1 (16 pages[11]):
Session 2: Chapter 2: The Building Blocks of RBA: (22 pages):
Session 3: Chapter 3: Population Accountability: (26 pages):
Session 4: Run the Population Turn the Curve Exercise in TH Appendix E
Session 5: Performance Accountability: (32 pages)
Session 6: Run the Performance Turn the Curve Exercise in TH Appendix E
Session 7: Chapter 5: Putting Population and Performance together: (7 pages)
Session 8: Chapter 6: Management Budgeting and Strategic Planning as a
        Single system: (21 pages)
Session 9. Chapter 7: Implementation Issues and Challenges, Closing and
        Epilogue: (26 pages)

In each session the agenda should be pretty simple. "What did you learn?" "How could we use this?" The essays in this Companion Reader could be used in the same way. Choose one or more topics to be read ahead of the meeting and use the same discussion questions.

There are a few different ways that a book-club like this might form. You generally don't want more than 10 or 15 people in the group. A manager trying to introduce these concepts might ask some or all members of the senior staff to participate. A group of peers from different organizations might come together to do this. If the discussions are honest, open and respectful, then the group could have the added benefit of building relationships and engaging new partners.

22. HONORING THE LEGACY OF PREVIOUS WORK

When working with RBA, it is NOT necessary to throw out all previous work and start over. In fact it is essential that you do NOT do this. It is essential that you honor previous work. This can be done in a few simple ways.

• With regard to data, first separate population indicators from performance measures. Then sort the previously identified performance measures into the three RBA categories: *How much did we do? How well did we do it? Is anyone better off?*

• With regard to analysis of conditions and causes, place those in the *story behind the curves.*

---

[11] Page counts are approximate.

- With regard to action plans and strategies place them in the *what works* or action plan sections of RBA.

All work that has previously been done fits somewhere in the RBA framework. The left hand column of the Crosswalk Tool (TH Appendix D) provides a good set of sorting categories. What you will find is that organizing the work this way makes it easier for people to understand how the elements of the work fit together. It makes it possible to build on previous work.

We have all had experience with the throw-it-out-and-start-over approach. There may be some rare instances where this is necessary. But the people you are working with are smart. They often know where they are trying to go. The job of RBA is to help them get there. Start by honoring the work they have already done.

23. HONORING CYNICISM

How do we deal with the cynics who just don't want to do this? My view has always been to honor cynicism. There is such a long history of false starts with this kind of work, it is only natural for people to be at least a little cynical. I know that I was when I worked in government.

When people are critical, when they complain, and ask hostile questions, don't get angry. Don't get defensive. Take a deep breath. Don't answer the criticism right away. Instead, have a conversation. Talk about what they mean when they say "unrealistic, or any other important word or phrase from what they said. Why do they feel this way? In 90% of the cases, there is some misunderstanding that you can address. If the conversation is taking too much time away from the group, pause it by inviting the person to talk at the break or at the end of the day. There is a good chance that whatever question is being asked is on the minds of others in the group. If you are respectful to critics, it shows everyone else that it is a safe place for them to ask their questions.

Here are some of the most common objections I have met with, and short notes on some possible answers.

> **You can't measure what I do.** You're right. We can't and shouldn't try to measure everything you do. Measurement is only one way of knowing how well we're doing. We also need to report on our accomplishments and tell the stories about the people whose lives we have touched. But there is almost always something that can be measured that is worth knowing. RBA can help you figure out what that something is. If you are curious about the effects of your work, you will want to get this data. It can help you get better at what you do. And it can help you tell the story of your work to funders and others in you community.

The data will be used against us. You're right to be worried about this. There is a long history of data being used for punishment. It is reasonable to worry about unfair treatment. But this attitude can cut us off from using data for our own purposes. The first purpose of data is to improve our performance, not to fill out forms and reports for other people. If necessary, look at your most important data in private, figure out what is going on and what you need to do. You will then be in a better position to tell the story of your performance to the outside world. It is often helpful to put that story into three parts: "Here's what we're doing well. Here's where we're not doing as well as we would like. And here's what we're doing to get better." If there is a case where data is used against you, then knowing the story behind the data and having an action plan already in place can be your best defense.

RBA is not rigorous evaluation. RBA is simplistic. RBA is a disciplined form of "self-evaluation" or continuous improvement that is accessible to everyone. RBA makes use of the findings from rigorous formal research and evaluation in two places: the *story behind the curve* and *what works* to do better. In both cases we need the best information the research community can provide about both causes and solutions. If you think RBA is simplistic, reserve judgment until you have tried the Turn the Curve exercise on an indicator or performance measure that you care about. The simplicity of RBA is deceptive. It is a powerful way to organize important conversations. Just be careful that the action plan you come up with is not simplistic. Complex problems will require complex solutions.

In the end, if the person is still dissatisfied or even angry, you can say some version of this: "If you are really worried about this work, then don't do it." This can be a little awkward if the organization sponsoring the workshop has "adopted" RBA. But don't let that hold you back from this answer. Whether you are in a training or leadership role, let people off the hook, at least for now. "OK, we'll leave you or your program out of this for now. We can come back and revisit this with you down the road. I want to make sure we address your concerns as much as possible." This is not a defeat. This just means you have a challenge. And it is worth being patient. In almost every case, people who feel they have been heard and treated respectfully will be more open to change.

24. A LESSON IN COACHING (strange interlude)

One of the sports channels recently showed a special called "A Football Life: Bill Belichick," about the coach of the New England Patriots. Belichick is one of the most successful and controversial coaches in American "football" history.

There is a scene right before the 2009 championship game with Baltimore where Belichick is standing at a podium before his assembled players. As part of a much longer monologue, he says, "I want you to understand how one stupid play, one stupid penalty, one stupid mistake ends it[12] for all of us." This is a hall-of-fame[13] management mistake. Putting pressure on people to "not make mistakes" almost never works. This is an amazing amount of pressure to add to the already pressure-packed life of a professional athlete. And what happened? The Patriots got clobbered by Baltimore 33-14. Did Belichick learn anything from this? Apparently not. In 2013, they got clobbered again by Baltimore 28 to 13.

What's the lesson? Maybe it's this: If you pressure people to not make mistakes, they will act cautiously and perform below their potential. Mistakes are part of learning. Risks are necessary for excellence. Make it clear to your best people that you will back them up if they make a mistake in the course of a good faith effort.

One day when I was CFO in the Maryland Department of Human Resources, I had a budget analyst come in to me terribly upset because he had made a $1 million dollar mistake in constructing his part of the budget. This was late in the budget process and the mistake could not be fixed. He was one of my best analysts. So I told him about the "Million Dollar Club" for people who have made million dollar mistakes, and that I was a charter member. And this was true. On a number of occasions I had misjudged a situation in a way that left the department with less money than we needed. I think my overall average was pretty good, but that kind of mistake came with the territory. In our $1 billion dollar plus budget, $1 million was less than one-tenth of one percent - still important, but not the end of the world. The analyst learned his lesson about being more careful. And the other analysts saw how he was treated. I didn't need to say anything. I don't think there was another such incident. The Million Dollar Club message was this: "If you have a complicated job that you perform well, it's not the end of the world if you occasionally make a mistake. The rest of us will back you up." Hear that Bellichek?

25. WHY NO-COST/LOW-COST IDEAS ARE SO IMPORTANT

There are important reasons why identifying and implementing no-cost/low-cost ideas are worth the effort.

---

[12] It's the last game of the season.

[13] What about the idea of a Management Hall of Fame. It would feature the best and worst of administrators and their behaviors over the years. It would give deserved recognition to examples of outstanding management, and put into perspective the foibles routinely portrayed in the news as common practice. It could also be a Center for Excellence in Management, with ties to organizational development experts and practitioners....and serve as a home for iconic work in this field, like Stephen Covey's "The 7 Habits of Highly Effective People", and Jim Collins "Good to Great."

- It helps make the case for funding. Funders love it when you are making the best use of your available resources. This makes your request for new funding more credible and more likely to be approved.

- It opens up otherwise closed channels of creativity. We have been trained to think that the answer to all problems is more money for more service. In fact there are many actions you and your partners can take that don't require new resources.

- No-cost/low-cost actions can usually be done quickly and often produce quick wins. These "wins" are good in their own right. But they also help to keep people engaged in the process and encourage the belief that the larger longer term progress we hope for is possible.

- It counters the excuse that "we can't do anything without more money." This is the number one excuse why people give up on change processes. It is almost never true. There are lots of things you and your partners can do while you go after the monetary resources you need.

- Thinking about no-cost/low-cost options opens up the action planning process to non-conventional partners. We need as many partners as we can get. The power of the community working together is one of your greatest potential assets. Asking for and acting on no-cost/low-cost ideas invites everyday citizens to be part of the process. It makes the process more inclusive and more effective.

I have been a fan over the years of Asset Based Community Development (ABCD), particularly the way it can be useful in the story behind the curve and thinking about what works and action plans.

Dan Duncan recently introduced me to some of the tools used in ABCD to develop action plans. There is one in particular you may want to use. It is the People, Power, Change game developed by Cormac Russell. We often believe that the solutions to problems confronting people and their communities require professional interventions and government programs. However, there are many things that people can do themselves and in fact there are many things that only people can do. Consider a community problem or a curve you are trying to turn. The three key questions are below. The first two can be a good source of no-cost / low cost ideas.

- What can only citizens do?
- What can only people do together with government and professionals?
- What can only government & professionals do?

Here is the link to Cormac Russell's website: nurturedevelopment.org

26. TRANSLATING RBA
(Thanks to Sabine Stoelb, Ilka Meisel, and Marie-Ange Schimmer)

Parts of RBA have now been translated from English into at least 10 other languages including Spanish, Swedish, Norwegian, Dutch, Hebrew, German, French, Te Reo Maori, Mandarin and Welsh.

The process of translation brings up a range of interesting challenges. Here's one important example. Recently my friends in Europe have been discussing the best way to translate the performance measurement category *Is anyone better off?*. In an entry below, I discuss the rationale behind this particular phrasing and explain why I have resisted certain proposed alternatives in English. But I agreed to the following sentence for the French and German translations: **"Has anyone or anything improved?"**

The phrase "better off" is a somewhat quirky English expression. There is a close equivalency between better off and improvement. And the use of the word "anyone" is tied to the notion of customers. We are accustomed to thinking about customers as people. But work with infrastructure services, like transportation, have made it clear that customers can sometimes be inanimate objects, like roads and bridges. (See the essay on infrastructure as customers in Chapter 3.) The percentage of bridges in good condition is an important measure for the agency responsible for monitoring and maintaining bridges. Obviously, the implied customers here are also the people using the bridge. And there are definitely measures for these customers too. The percentage of time the bridge is closed or restricted for unscheduled maintenance is a direct measure of the convenience of its use by motorists and pedestrians. So the phrasing "anyone or anything" reflects this difference in an unambiguous way that is the closest match we can find to the nuance of "Is anyone better off?" in English.

The most important caution in translating this particular phrase is not to introduce the idea of "causality," as in "Have we caused anyone or anything to improve?" or "How much change did we produce?" Causality is complex. It involves many factors and many players and is difficult and often impossible to know. The only way to have any certainty about causality is research and even research is often inconclusive on this point. So it is best not to construct measurement categories that assert causality. In RBA, it is always better to think in terms of **contribution**.

*28. MENTAL MODELS (Appendix F)

Reading Senge's *The Fifth Discipline* got me thinking again about mental models. His contention is that they are not so much the object of change efforts as they are obstacles that stand in the way of change. The first task is to identify what mental models are holding us back. Appendix F lists of some of the current mental models and the ones we would like to see take their place. This is a combination of RBA concepts and leadership concepts in no particular order. Thanks to John Ott, David Burnby and Jolie Bain Pillsbury for their help in developing this list. There are certainly more than these. Suggested additions are welcome.

*28. HOW TO USE THE RBA SELF ASSESSMENT (Appendix G)

The RBA/OBA Self Assessment Questionnaire (SAQ) has been significantly revised since its publication in the original 2005 edition of TH. It is much more detailed and complete, and it includes a scoring methodology, which we'll come to in a minute.

The first, and in some respects most important, use of the RBA/OBA Self Assessment Questionnaire (SAQ) is as an implementation checklist. An organization could (should) periodically go through this list to see which of these things are being done. A simplified score could be computed as the percentage of SAQ items that are being done at all. There are 18 items listed. What percentage of the 18 are completed or in process?

The item-by-item scoring built into the SAQ is an add-on to this process that allows organizations to assess how they are doing on each item and create an overall composite implementation score. The score for each item is derived using the maximum points in parentheses after each item, and judging how far along you are in earning that maximum.

The overall composite score is calculated by adding together the item-by-item scores. (The three score adjustments at the bottom are optional.) This can then be plotted on a baseline and used in a turn-the-curve process.

There is no established good score. Even though the scale runs from zero to 100, it can not be interpreted the way we do in education. A better way to think about the SAQ composite score is in terms of the progressive use of RBA. The scale below is one example:

  0 - 20 Beginning to use RBA
  21 - 40 Well along in implementing RBA
  41 - 60 Developing expertise in RBA implementation
  61 - 80 Moderately expert in RBA implementation
  81 - 100 Expert in RBA implementation

Note that the SAQ in its current form is designed for organizations that deliver services and not for population level community partnerships. It is possible to use the current version for such partnerships by considering the subset of questions applicable to your work.

CHAPTER 2:
Population Accountability

Population Accountability is about the well-being of our people. We want, for example, "Healthy People, Safe Communities, and A Clean and Sustainable Environment." How can we start with these ambitions and work backward to actions we need to take now? I think it is fair to say that we have not been trained to think this way. I can speak for myself from twenty years of working in government. We had our hands full administering and delivering services. Quality of life seemed like a far-off distraction. Of course we saw quality of life referenced in articles and political processes. But the idea of starting with a specific articulation of quality of life, such as "People Live in Safe, Stable, Affordable Housing," and working backward to actions rarely if ever happened. In our rush to solutions, we skipped, and still skip, the most important steps necessary for impact[14] on quality of life. What are the Indicators, the Story behind the Indicators, the Partners who can help. What works?, What could work?, and **What would it take?**

*1. HOW TO MEASURE THE SUCCESS OF POPULATION LEVEL STRATEGIES OR INITIATIVES

The general population level progression from results to indicators to baselines, story, partners, *what works* and strategies, often leads people to ask next, "What performance measures will tell us if our strategies are working?" This is the **wrong** question. To tell whether a population level strategy is working, we must look to see if the INDICATOR curves are turning. Indicators measure the extent to which population strategies are working. Performance measures tell us if the service and other components of our strategies are working. This is a very common misunderstanding.

For example, a partnership might come together to promote community safety as measured by indicators such as the crime rate or the percentage of people who feel safe walking in their neighborhood. After working through the RBA process, they might settle on an initial three part strategy which includes community policing, improved

---

[14] As you will see from the next essay, I am a fan of Collective Impact and the work of John Kania, Mark Kramer and many others in this worldwide conversation.

lighting and a neighborhood watch program. To see if the overall strategy is working, we would look to see if the curves are turning on the crime rate and the percentage of people who feel safe. For performance measures, we would take each component of the strategy in turn and identify measures for that component. So for the neighborhood watch program, we might look at the percentage of neighbors signed up, or the crime rate for neighborhoods in the program compared to comparable neighborhoods not in the program.

There is one other kind of performance measure relevant here, which may be a source of some of the confusion. For those managing the overall strategic effort, there is a need to know the extent to which the strategy or strategies are being implemented and how well they are being implemented. This requires performance measures suited to this purpose, such as the percentage of action steps within a strategy that are on track, on time and on budget. For those managing the partnership, it might be useful to know the percentage of partners actively contributing. Notice how these **performance** measures allow us to grasp the complex details of implementing a strategy, not the success of the strategy itself.

We need to know both things. We need to know if our overall strategy is working (population indicators) and whether strategy implementation is working (performance measures). It is possible to have a strategy that is implemented beautifully, but has no effect on the indicators. RBA is a self-correcting process but only if population and performance are maintained in their proper relationship.

*2. COLLECTIVE IMPACT USING RBA (Appendix II)

Collective Impact and RBA are a perfect fit. The idea of working together to make a difference at the community level is at the heart of both bodies of work. And RBA complements Collective Impact in other ways. Collective Impact literature sets out conditions for the success of community change efforts, and RBA provides specific methods that partners can use to meet those conditions.

More and more places are describing their work in terms of implementing Collective Impact using RBA. In 2011, Deitre Epps from the Results Leadership Group authored an excellent analysis of the relationship between Collective Impact and RBA, entitled "Achieving 'Collective Impact' with Results-Based Accountability™" (available on the Results Leadership Group website).

Appendix H is a short summary of how to use RBA to achieve Collective Impact, that is a supplement to, not replacement for, Deitre's excellent work. Feel free to copy it. It is now a common workshop handout. I hope you find it useful.

*3. CO-CONSPIRATORS

If you look at any success story where people have actually turned a curve, you will always find a core group of what I like to call "co-conspirators." These are the handful of people who are determined to make things happen, come hell or high water, with or without money, with or without permission, and with or without recognition. The cast of characters around the core group varies over time. Allies and enemies come and go (although the enemies tend to stay). But the co-conspirators are the constant that produces change. It is important to remember that you only need one other person to get started. The two of you will then be much more successful at recruiting numbers 3, 4 etc. Sometimes the next partner to recruit will be obvious. Sometimes it will take a little detective work.

This is really just an operational version of the famous Margaret Meade quote: "Never doubt that a small group of thoughtful, committed citizens can change the world. Indeed, it is the only thing that ever has." My favorite example of this is Mothers Against Drunk Driving which started in 1980 with five women in the back of a restaurant. It is now an international movement with at least one critically important turned curve to show. So if someone asks you what they need to do to turn a curve they really care about, the first question you should ask is "Who are your co-conspirators?"

*4. MULTIPLE LISTS OF POPULATION RESULTS - AND WHAT TO DO

What can you do when there are multiple co-existing sets of population results or outcomes in a given jurisdiction? It is an increasingly common problem. One or more agencies (local, state or national) adopt a set of results/outcomes without regard to others that may already have been established.

First, it is worth noting that this is a good sign. If people are creating results/outcomes lists, it means that the concept of population results/outcomes is meaningful to a range of people who have been able to adapt it to their own circumstances. Consider this in contrast to a single rigid set of results/outcomes imposed on people from the top. When this has been done (and it has been) the list is resented and not used.

However, the existence of multiple sets of results/outcomes at the population level FEELS uncomfortable and chaotic to those of us who are prone to like things in order. Time to pull out the Zen Management Handbook. It's OK. Relax.

There may be an advantage to creating a core population list. Figure 2 shows one place where this was done for the Alaska Mental Health Trust Authority. At the time of this work, MHTA was responsible for four very different sub-populations or beneficiary groups[15]. Quality of life ambitions were articulated for each of these populations. The chart at the right places the four different population results lists around the outside. We then identified the common elements in the middle. This structure was used for deciding on a set of common results, while maintaining respect for the original separate results. This enabled the best of both worlds, a core set of results and separately adapted lists for different sub-populations.

It is more common to have two, not four, separate lists. A similar approach can be used. Lay the different lists side by side, with a blank column in the middle, and look for commonalities. Chances are it will be easy to see how elements in one list correspond to one or more elements in the other list(s). It might be possible to create a crosswalk to show how the lists could be edited to conform more closely. It might be possible to get people to agree on merging the lists. This can be politically difficult but it has been done in a few places.

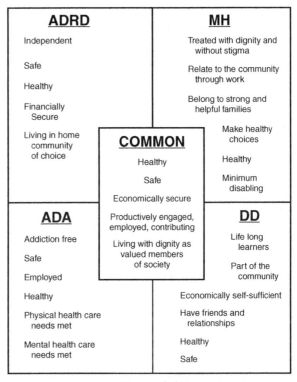

Alaska Mental Health Trust Authority

Results for Beneficiaries: 9/22/97 Working Session

Figure 2.1

The ideal situation is, of course, a clean slate. When Georgia established a list of 5 population results (and 26 indicators) for children and families in the early 1990's it accompanied it with a very important policy. The 150 local Family Connections Partnerships were required to use the list, BUT they could add to the list to reflect local priorities AND they could subtract from or modify the list if they had a compelling reason to do so. Some counties added to the list. No one to my knowledge ever subtracted from it. But the offer of the possibility to add, subtract or change showed respect for local people. And even if the option is not used, this respect may be one of the most important factors determining whether the work will succeed or fail.

---

[15] mhtrust.org/about/beneficiaries

In the UK we have a number of examples of local councils such as Leeds and Hull, adding to or changing the list of Every Child Matters (ECM) outcomes included in the Children Act of 2004. Portsmouth, under the leadership of Rob Hutchinson[16], was one of the first councils to develop a list of outcomes, well before ECM. In each case, leaders could show the crosswalk to ECM outcomes, while continuing to use their own lists.

The lessons here are simple. Work toward a unified list if possible, but allow different lists to peacefully coexist. Make sure any jurisdiction-wide list has a safety valve policy (like Georgia's) to allow variations where needed. Don't wait for or ask for permission to create your own list where it is needed.

5. Review: *POOR ECONOMICS* by Abhijit V. Banerjee and Esther Duflo

Thanks to David Brett for putting me on to the book "Poor Economics: A Radical Rethinking of the Way to Fight Global Poverty" by Abhijit V. Banerjee and Esther Duflo. This is a must read for anyone interested in reducing poverty in their community city, county, council, state or nation.

The book is filled with examples of what works to improve economic outcomes, health outcomes, education outcomes and more, all the essential components of any serious attack on poverty. Most of the ideas in the book have been tested with Random Control Trials (RCT's) in poor countries. But it is a mistake to think these lessons apply only to poor countries. Many of these ideas can be fruitfully applied in "developed" countries as well. The book endorses the mantra "Nothing about us without us," asserting that any successful change effort must be planned with, not imposed on, the community.

One of the great gifts of this book is its relentless insistence on setting aside stereotypes of the poor and looking at how poor people actually live, how and why they make choices, and what those realities mean for policy. They do this not just from the survey of relevant research but from years of actual work in the field. In RBA terms, this is a deep dive into the *story behind the curve*.

One of the examples concerned the distribution of repellant treated mosquito nets as a way to prevent malaria. One of the many ideologies driving the design of poverty reduction programs is the notion that market forces can be aligned to support the right thing to do. This often plays out well when it comes to micro-enterprise. So researchers tested the idea of market distribution of mosquito nets vs. free distribution. It turned

---

[16] Rob Hutchinson and Mike Pinnock were the ones who first introduced OBA to the UK in 1999.

out free distribution got more nets to more people and thereby prevented more malaria. Even the low cost of nets in the market model kept the poorest people from getting them. You will find this way of testing conventional wisdom throughout the book.

Almost all of the examples in the book are carefully designed single interventions, like this one, in part because funders prefer interventions that are relatively easy to evaluate. This is OK. We need as much information as we can get on research-proven practice. RBA makes use of this information in the *What works* step of the talk to action process. But there are no examples in the book of anything like the RBA thinking process itself, where you start with one or more results and indicator curves and work backward to a set of strategies to Turn the Curve(s). If this is done well, the strategy will include contributions from an array of partners. These kinds of strategies are not stable single interventions. They change, they grow, they improve over time. Such strategies are not suited to RCT evaluation because you can't isolate which components produced which effects. (See the discussion of evidence above and TH pp. 131-133 / pp. 136-139).

The best part of the book is the authors' break with the lazy pessimism entrenched in the economics community that nothing really works and nothing can be done. They present a wealth of tested ideas that can make a difference even in politically dysfunctional societies. The book is filled with stories that will stay with you. If you are working on reducing poverty, or even if you're not, read this book.

6. WHEN CAN PERFORMANCE MEASURES FOR A SERVICE POPULATION BE USED AS INDICATORS FOR A WHOLE POPULATION?

Consider "All children with identified disabilities in city X." Is this a subpopulation within Population Accountability or a service population? Well first and foremost, it's a service population since some organization must have done the identifying. Let's say the organization (school, health organization etc.) did a good job and successfully identified 90% of all children with disabilities. In this case the service population is very close in size to the total population, and any performance measures associated with this group (e.g. percentage who get needed treatment, percentage who achieve reading proficiency etc.) could be one of those indicators that plays a double role as both a service system performance measure, and a population indicator.

But what if only 10% of the children with disabilities have been identified? First off, any performance measures associated with service for this group would not be representative of the conditions of "All children with disabilities" and should probably not be used as a population indicator. Secondly, it is very important to know approximately what this percentage is. *The percent of children successfully identified* is a *How well?* performance measure. This is similar to the *percent of need met,* an important *How well?* measure for any service targeted to an under-served population, or any service that meets only a portion of known need (e.g. child care services).

This scenario also raises the question, Why not create a quality of life report card for persons with disabilities as a Population Accountability effort? If done right this could be a valuable advocacy tool and vehicle for organizing action to improve conditions. It would draw on data from the service system, but also from census data and possibly specially designed surveys. Release of such reports draws press coverage and provides an opportunity to raise public awareness about conditions that might not be OK. These same kind of considerations apply to any important subpopulation in our communities by race, ethnicity or physical and mental condition.

7. WHEN CAN A SECTOR WORKFORCE BE CONSIDERED A POPULATION?

Are all doctors in New Zealand a population under Population Accountability or a service system workforce under Performance Accountability? Technically any group of workers are employees of the service system within which they work, the health care system in this case. The percentage of doctors who have special training in recognizing child abuse and domestic violence, would be an important *How well did we do it?* measure for the health care service system. So it is generally a good idea to first consider any group that is defined by having a client or service role as part of Performance Accountability.

However, we know that service systems lie at the boundary between Population and Performance Accountability. And not all professions are well organized into clearly identifiable systems within which to place performance measures. The percentage of all people in the "driving profession" (e.g. taxi drivers, bus drivers, truck drivers etc.) who have untreated vision problems might work better as a population indicator (perhaps of community safety) rather than a performance measure for a loosely defined transportation service system. Consider other possible professions (construction workers, barbers, shepherds etc.). So, whenever you are working in grey areas where something might fit into more than one category, **the dictating principle is utility**. Which perspective is most useful to the work you are trying to do?

8. A SHORTCUT METHOD FOR CHOOSING POPULATION INDICATORS

The "regular" method presented in TH (pp. 54 - 56 / 55 - 57)involves rating each potential measure "high, medium or low" on three criteria: Communication Power, Proxy Power and Data Power. There is a simpler method for doing this that mirrors steps 4 and 5 in choosing performance measures in TH Appendix G.

The following method is used after you have finished brainstorming all possible indicators for a given population result.

Go through the list of potential indicators and identify those for which you currently have good data. Put a circle next to these measures. Then ask "If you had to stand up in a public place and explain to your neighbors what you mean by (the result in question, e.g. Healthy Children), and could only use one of the measures with a circle next to it, which one would you use?" Then ask, "What if you could have a second.... a third?" Through this method you can identify the top three indicators for any given result. As circumstances dictate, you can go beyond three if that is useful.

This method is faster and easier, and is exactly equivalent to the Communication - Proxy - Data method. By first identifying the measures for which you have good data, you address Data Power. By asking which would be your first choice in a public place, you force participants to consider Communication and Proxy power together, namely, which measures are most powerful that people will understand?

This method also sets up the creation of a Data Development Agenda. Again, paralleling the performance process, ask "If we could buy one of the measures for which we don't have data, the ones without the circles, which would be the first one we would buy?" "What if we could buy a second, a third...?" Through this process you can create both headline measures and a prioritized list of where you need new or better data.

9. WHY POPULATION ACCOUNTABILITY SHOULD BE IMPORTANT TO K-12[17] EDUCATORS

I make the case in TH (p. 52 / 53) that Early Childhood Education (ECE) advocates will be more successful if they argue for ECE as a necessary part of a larger strategy to get all children ready for school. Receipt of ECE service is not an end-in-itself but rather one component of this strategy, along with support for parents, living wage jobs, qual-

---

[17] K-12, or Kindergarten to High School Grade 12 is also referred to as Primary and Secondary education.

ity health care etc. Traditional advocacy states by contrast that "all children deserve a high quality ECE experience." You can easily see the difference. The power of a contribution relationship to quality of life versus entitlement to a high quality service. Recognizing services as a means to higher ends places advocacy on a more sound footing and is more likely to garner popular and political support. This view has now spread through the ECE community, partly as a result of national, state and local efforts devoted to school readiness.

The higher education community has also gotten this message and has gradually shifted its advocacy emphasis to workforce preparation and its contribution to creating a "Competitive 21st Century Economy."

But K-12 (Primary - Secondary) education too often seems to miss out on these connections. This is due in part to the social and political assault on education in the US, including the devaluation of teachers, cuts in education funding, and a definition of success based on test scores. It is not surprising that education advocacy these days is more defense than offence. The advocates for education traditionally argue that education is a good in itself. "We need to provide a high quality education for all students." And YES, we do.

But why? Why do we need education at all? We need to remember the public good that education is intended to promote. Young people prepared to succeed in life. Young people prepared to support themselves and their families. And, often forgotten, Young people prepared to be good citizens. The public is tired of, and largely disconnected from, the controversies about curriculum and teacher evaluation. What if we went back to basics and re-sold education for the quality of life conditions it can help create, and tracked the indicators of those conditions to see if we are turning any curves?

I think this conversation is worth having, particularly for those immersed in the day to day management of the K-12 system. It shows that the education system is not responsible for curing the ills of society. By stepping back and thinking about the role of education in society and its contribution to quality of life, we have a chance to get back to our shared values, and to remember why our large monetary investments in education are worth every penny and more. And maybe we can begin to re-conceptualize education as more than a set of services and instead a community enterprise to which everyone has something to contribute.

CHAPTER 3:
Performance Accountability

Performance Accountability is about how well programs, agencies and service systems are working. This is sometimes a more important and urgent subject than Population Accountability for the simple reason that most people work in organizations that deliver services. In this chapter we explore some lessons that come from implementing the performance ideas presented in TH.

*1. BUILD A PERFORMANCE FOUNDATION IN YOUR ORGANIZATION

If you are facing the challenge of getting a medium size or large organization to start using performance measures, there is a great temptation to issue a mandate for all programs to start at once. Whether you use RBA or some other method, this approach is likely to fail. If you want any structure to last, you have to spend time and effort building a strong foundation. When it comes to performance measurement, that foundation is built program by program across the bottom of the organization chart. By program, I mean a manager and group of people who provide a particular service (e.g. Smoking Cessation program) or perform a particular set of functions (e.g. HR). The exact level of detail at this level will vary from agency to agency.

For each program, identify 3 to 5 Headline Measures from the *How well did we do it?* and *Is anyone better off?* categories. If you do this right, you will also identify Secondary Measures, and a Data Development Agenda. For any given program, a first cut at this can be done in about an hour using the 5-step process in TH Appendix G.[18]

Over time this three part list will be improved. But don't wait for it to be perfect. Take one of the 3 to 5 measures and run the Performance Turn the Curve Exercise right away (TH Appendix E). Give them the EXPERIENCE of USING performance measures to improve performance. See if they are willing to commit to having the Turn the Curve conversation for at least one of the measures on a monthly basis after you leave. Then go on to the next program, and the next. Start with managers who want to do this (see the 20-60-20 Rule below).

---

[18] Also available from the Publications page of the FPSI website resultsaccountability.com/publications.

If you visualize the organization chart as a triangle with programs at the bottom and progressive layers of management going up, when you work across the bottom of the triangle you literally build a performance foundation for everything above. This approach takes a lot more time than an all-at-once doomed-to-fail mandate. You might actually have to convince the chief executive to be patient. But like all good foundations, it will last.

Note that this is also the way to develop NATURAL commonalities in measurement across programs in contrast to the top-down measures chosen by the agency executives that often don't make sense when they reach the program level. These naturally common measures can then be used to identify the headline performance measures used at the division and total organizational levels. And they can point to natural opportunities for partnership across the organization.

*2. CHANGE THE FORMS, CHANGE THE CULTURE

If you have worked in a government or nonprofit organization for a long time, you may have noticed that the forms you use for budgeting, planning, procurement, etc. don't change very often. Sometimes they don't change for years or even decades. This suggests an interesting hypothesis that may be helpful in organizational change processes: that forms are the skeletal structure supporting organizational culture. So if you want to change organizational culture, one powerful way to do that is to change the forms.

Let's say, for talking purposes, that you want to get people to consider the contribution of their program to population quality of life. What if you put a section at the beginning of the budget form where people had to say in a sentence or two how their program contributes to quality of life? What if you wanted them to show the three most important performance measures in baseline form? What if you wanted them to show the story behind the baselines, or how their improvement action plan connects to their budget request? All of this is possible with relatively simple changes to the forms used for performance reporting, budgeting and strategic planning.

Similar changes could be used to implement Next Generation Contracting provisions (see below) by changing procurement forms, and more importantly the boilerplate sections of contracts. What if those contracts called for the negotiation of the 3 to 5 most important performance measures (from *How well did we do it?* and *Is anyone better off?)?* What if the contract required the contractor to have a continuous improvement process (e.g. monthly consideration of the RBA 7 Performance Accountability questions)? What if the contract said that the contract monitor would meet with the contractor at least 3 times a year to discuss performance and work in partnership with the contractor to help improve their performance? Forms are powerful tools, that can be harnessed in the service of organizational change. And the changes you make, for better or worse, could last for decades.

*3. THE MISUSE OF TARGETS

Here is an example of how targets can become meaningless and even dangerous. Consider the following display of a safety rating score for an imaginary airline, Safety First Airlines. It is made up of two years of actuals (2014 and 2015), the current year estimate (2016) where the end-of-year actual is not yet known, and "targets" for 2017, 2018 and 2019.

SAFETY FIRST AIRLINES
Average Annual Safety Rating

2014 Actual	2015 Actual	2016 Estimated Actual	2017 Target	2018 Target	2019 Target
7.9	8.0	8.1	8.2	8.3	8.4

Figure 3.1

What does this picture tell us? It shows the rating going up from 2014 to 2016, from 7.9 to 8.1. The targets suggest that the progress will continue from 2017 to 2019 from 8.2 to 8.4. But wait a minute! Would you want to fly on an airline with an 8.4 safety rating? Of course not. A target is something you strive for. 8.4 is not a target. It is a contrivance to fill out the form so you can maintain the picture of steady progress through the coming budget process. The targets are set low enough that you are likely to achieve them without doing much if anything more than you are doing now.

When it comes to safety, the real target is 10.0. But the Airline's monthly management report is designed to show the percentage of targets met. If your targets are set too high, you will be embarassed and maybe punished. So the incentive is to keep it safe.

When it is not something as important as an airline safety rating, this kind of display can put people to sleep. "OK, they plan to make progress. That's good. Next budget." If the problem with an 8.4 target occurs to them, the conversation is likely to be about blame and not how to improve.

Why are your targets so low?
Why aren't you more ambitious?
Why aren't you working harder?

Would this display be any better if we set all the 2017-2019 targets to 10.0? Of course not. No one would believe it. It would still be a conversation disconnected from the reality of what is happening and what it would take to get better.

Of course, an airline would never actually work this way.... would it? But there are countless examples of this kind of thinking and this kind of display in public budgeting and planning.

Imagine that we created a different way for the airline to show safety scores.

SAFETY FIRST AIRLINES
Average Annual Safety Rating

2014 Actual	2015 Actual	2016 Estimated Actual	2017	2018	2019	Aspirational Target
			Baseline Forecast			
7.9	8.0	8.1	8.2	8.3	8.4	10.0

Figure 3.2

There are two changes in this display. First, the 2017 to 2019 columns are no longer labeled as targets. They are labeled as "Baseline Forecast." The forecast is where we are headed with current policy, procedures and resources. Nothing about the word "forecast" signals that these are desired or acceptable levels. They are simply the best guess about what the future looks like if we don't do something more or different than what we are doing now. If this forecast is accepted by the organization, then it must be owned by the organization. And changes necessary to improve become a common enterprise, not a matter of isolated responsibility and blame.

The second change is the addition of a new column for "Aspirational Target." This target has no date attached. This target is one we want to get as close to as possible, as soon as possible. With this display we can have a more useful conversation.

"Why is the forecast for 2017 to 2019 only 8.2 to 8.4?"
"What is causing this?"
"What resources or other changes are needed if we want to get to 10.0?"
"What do we need to do right away?"

See how the concept of target is meaningless in the first display and meaningful in the second. The point is that targets can and should be used when they are fair and useful. Most targets are neither fair nor useful. They are not fair because they are set too high and are not achievable. Or they are set too low so they can be safely met. They generate game-playing behavior and not aspirational behavior. In these cases, targets are not just meaningless, but can actually be dangerous.

The lesson is this: Make sure that they are not used for punishment but rather as a way to encourage people to strive to do better. And do all of your planning with data using baselines with history and forecast.

How does this compare to the way your organization arrays its budget information and uses targets?

*4. TIPS FOR DEVELOPING STRONG PERFORMANCE IMPROVEMENT PLANS (or how to get the most out of the Turn the Curve thinking process)

There are two separate steps within the RBA/OBA talk to action thinking process that directly support the development of action plans. The paragraphs below address some specific ways of using these two steps in developing performance improvement plans. The process is very similar for Population Accountability. The starting point is one or more important performance measure baselines where the forecast is "not OK."

The Story Behind the Baseline: This is where we usually ask people to tell us what they believe are the causes and forces at work behind the numbers. This will usually generate a useful discussion. But there is a sharper way to frame this question that can be helpful, particularly for processes that get stuck. Ask about the customers (clients or service users) for whom the service did NOT work. If the service worked for 80% of its customers on a given measure, then who are the 20% for whom it did not work? Why didn't it work for those particular people? Don't settle for easy answers. Get into the specifics. Use the Information and Research Agenda between turn-the-curve sessions to review individual case records. If some customers dropped out and failed to complete the program, talk to a few of them to find out why.

> [REMEMBER that when having any kind of follow-up contact with a customer, the principle purpose **must not** be data gathering. The first purpose of finding out why someone dropped out, for example, is to see if there is "anything we can do to get you to come back, or any other way we can help you?" Data gathering is always a byproduct of these other questions. This means that you should put your very best people on these types of follow-up calls.]

Take each cause for why the service hasn't worked and ask what could be done to address that particular cause in the future. This will generate a list of possible action steps, including *no-cost/low-cost* ideas. Not all of these will be great ideas, but everything goes on the potential shopping list for now.

The Partners who could help: Brainstorm a list of partners who have a role to play in doing better. Push the discussion beyond the usual suspects to consider unconventional partners. Include people or agencies on the list even if they have been unhelpful in the past. Ask for "crazy ideas" about partners. THEN, go down the list of partners and ask how each particular partner could help. If they are not currently helping, ask what could be done to recruit or engage them. If the relationship with the potential partner is damaged, ask what could be done to repair the damage. Make sure that you don't allow the discussion to get into negatives. Have the discussion at a time and place (and in small enough groups) where people can relax and have an open exchange. If you can arrange it, have this discussion with some of your most trusted partners in the room. This can best be done, at least the first time, as part of a Turn the Curve exercise. The "not-OK" curve you are working to turn serves as a touchstone for each partner to see the importance of what you are doing and the connection to their own work. Having participants wear two hats helps identify what absent partners could do. This discussion will generate two types of possible actions: 1) actions that already engaged partners are willing to take, or at least bring "home" for consideration; and 2) actions you can take to engage absent or potential partners who have something important to contribute.

When talking to partners, it is a good idea to discuss how turning your curve can help the partner achieve the core mission of their agency. Partnerships are not always, or even mostly, about altruism. When agencies have customers in common, actions to improve one agency's service will often have beneficial effects for others.

These two steps will produce a "shopping list" from which actions can be chosen for implementation. The criteria for choosing which possible actions go in the action plan are discussed in TH (pp. 43-44 / 44 - 45). As the action plan is developed you will need a process for assigning responsibilities, creating timelines, and monitoring progress.

Finally a word about programs that are performing at a very high level and don't think they need to worry about performance improvement. In any complex system, static states rarely if ever exist. Your performance is either getting better or worse. If you are not trying to get better, chances are you're getting worse.

*5. PAY FOR PERFORMANCE HAS NO PLACE IN GOVERNMENT

In 2014, we learned about fraudulent performance reporting in the US Veteran's Administration (VA) health system. It was not surprising to learn that there were executive pay incentives attached to performance reporting. There is a long-standing view that government employees will do a better job if their good work is rewarded with private-sector-type bonuses. This is a DANGEROUS FALLACY.

Consider three things. 1) People don't go into government work to make a lot of money. They go because working for government is a good way to make a contribution to society. In my experience, most people in government work hard because it is THE RIGHT THING TO DO. 2) Studies have shown that financial rewards are fourth or fifth on the list of what motivates people. Higher on the list is a sense of accomplishment and recognition for good work. There are well-tested methods for employee recognition that should be part of every organization's culture. 3) And finally, financial rewards attached to performance ALWAYS create perverse incentives. Not just sometimes. ALWAYS (see the next essay below).

This is what we see playing out in the VA example. The right way to run an organization involves creating a culture where data is used first and foremost to understand and improve performance. Financial incentives are not just unnecessary, they are dangerous.

*6. REIMBURSEMENT BASED ON OUTCOMES ALWAYS CREATES PERVERSE INCENTIVES (Friedman's Law?)

Do not, I repeat, do NOT create reimbursement schemes based on outcomes. It is a trap. Well meaning people predictably fall into this trap every year. What is the bait that lures them in? It is the false equivalency of the government sector with the business sector. It is the notion that we can harness the profit motive to get programs to do the right thing for people. There is only one thing the profit motive can do and that is motivate people to make a profit.

Every time profit is attached to outcomes, whether population or performance, PERVERSE INCENTIVES ARE UNAVOIDABLY CREATED. The best you can then do is mitigate those incentives with checks and balances. And inevitably the checks and balances have loopholes that need to be fixed. And then the fixes have loopholes. This downward spiral creates more work and further distracts from the purpose of the work. The incentive for good work should be recognition for high levels of achievement on a balanced set of performance measures (from *How well did we do it?* and *Is anyone better off?*).

My favorite example of this is a case where a hospital was being judged (and therefore financially rewarded) for low in-patient death rates by type of operation. What they did should not be a surprise. If you were about to die, they discharged you. Their in-patient death rates looked great compared to other hospitals. But it actually signaled worse service for patients.

If you have any remaining doubts about the problems with government financial incentives, check out Chapter 7 of Rachel Maddow's book *Drift* for a full account of exactly how badly things went (and continue to go) with the Pentagon's privatization program. And check out "What you need to know about privatization," and "The pros and mostly cons of contingency fee contracting for revenue maximization" on the FPSI website publications list.

*7. NEXT GENERATION CONTRACTING (Appendix I and Appendix R)

If you run a nonprofit/NGO anywhere in the world, you are probably receiving funding from 10 or more funders all with different grant application and performance reporting requirements. You spend all your time running around meeting all these separate requirements and don't have time left to do the real job of running the agency. I believe funders have an obligation to get their act together. This means standardizing application, contracting and reporting requirements. Right now the relationship between funders and grantees is often a feudal relationship: overlord and serf. Funders can sit back and watch their grantees struggle and it's not their problem. We need to create a more co-equal relationship between funders and grantees, so that they work in partnership to produce the best possible results for their customers.

I have developed an agenda for how to reform contracts for funders and grantees (Appendix I). It lays out 10 steps including how funders and grantees can work together to develop the most important performance measures, how to work in partnership to maximize customer results, how the funding community can reform reporting requirements, switch to multiyear funding using rolling three year contracts, and create useful targets.

I am hopeful that these ideas will not seem so strange in five years. Visionary leaders are already adopting some of them. While they seem like common sense suggestions, it will take courage to put any of these ideas into action. We have seen a number of places begin this process including most recently the New Zealand Ministry for Business, Innovation and Employment. The press release in Appendix R provides a link to this work and a good summary of the breadth of RBA work in New Zealand.

*8. AN RBA EXPERT IN EVERY UNIT

Think about setting up an RBA network across your organization. The network can be used to promote good practice and can also provide a form of peer-based quality control. Here is a beginning plan for building organizational RBA capacity.

1. Ask each program to assign someone to become their in-house RBA expert. (Treat this like a technical support function like an in-house technology expert.)

2. Have these people practice and get good at selecting performance measures and running the Turn the Curve Exercises.

3. Create a network of these in-house experts so they can support each other, and learn how to do joint RBA training and coaching.

4. Ask the in-house experts to review the RBA Self-Assessment Questionnaire (and create a score if useful) on a regular basis.

5. Ask members of the network to train new people in RBA and mentor people who want to develop their RBA expertise.

If more than one organization does this in a jurisdiction, create a larger network linking the RBA efforts across organizations.

*9. DON'T TRY TO CONNECT PERFORMANCE MEASURES TO INDICATORS

There will be some situations where a program performance measure has a clear look-alike connection to a population indicator. For example, the "% of people who get jobs" in a job training program will relate directly to the population result "Prosperous Economy" and the indicator "rate of unemployment." But this is the exception and not the rule.

The vast majority of performance measures will **not** have a direct connection to a population indicator and that's OK. There is no need to directly connect performance measures to indicators. Instead each program should use narrative statements to explain how the program **contributes** to one or more population results or population outcomes.

This contribution relationship is more powerful and important than an elusive relationship between metrics. It can be stated for all programs and does not rely on the odd chance that a performance measure will "match" with an indicator.

The argument behind this proposition is just a matter of simple math. In any given jurisdiction there are not likely to be more than 50 to 100 established population indicators, while there will be hundreds of programs and thousands of performance measures in the government and nonprofit sectors. Forcing a thousand or more performance measures to link to only 50 or 100 population indicators assures that few such linkages will be meaningful. The narrative of contribution, however, works every time.

*10. THE CARDIFF AND VALE EXPERIENCE by Ruth Jordan,
with thanks also to Vicki Myson (Appendix J)

An RBA framework was introduced in South Wales in 2009 for the Welsh Epilepsy Unit in Cardiff. Staff members did an RBA exercise using the 7 Performance Accountability Questions for patients with a first suspected seizure or unexplained blackout. Within 2 hours, staff participants answered 6 of the 7 questions and at a follow-up meeting, answered the 7th question to create an action plan. Staff members then repeated the 7 questions for different subpopulations including women who might become pregnant, and people admitted to the hospital after a seizure. The staff members created an easy to read report card for each customer group, and data was collected every month. The impact of applying RBA was profound. The average length of time from seizure to diagnosis decreased from 111 days to 30 days and the average wait time to see a specialist decreased from 22 to 11 days.

The Epilepsy Unit deserves a lot of credit for this work! It is a great story about dedicated people using RBA to improve their services, including at least four turned curves! The form they developed for reporting is simply brilliant and the best I have seen anywhere. It can be used or adapted for any program. It has all the right elements: a description of the service and its customers (including contribution to quality of life), the most important performance measure baselines, the story behind the baselines, partners who can help, and the summary of an action plan.

It provides a perfect agenda for staff to meet, once a week/month/quarter to discuss how the service is doing and how to do better. Why not use this form to report on your services? Then fill out all the funder's required forms and put them in an appendix AFTER your version of the Epilepsy Unit report. A second appendix can contain any "overflow" detail you think is worth including that doesn't fit on the one page form. This room for overflow information could be important during the transition to simpler reporting when it might be harder to let go of all of the detail. See if this doesn't produce some immediate benefits in terms of the clarity and focus of the work, and an eventual reduction in paperwork.

See Appendix J for the full report about this extraordinary work.

*11. THE 20-60-20 RULE

In any organizational change process, 20% of the people will go along and give it a try. 60% will eventually follow along behind. The other 20% will never do it no matter what you do. You can spend all of your time as a manager on the 20% who will never do it. You can even spend all of your time on the 60% who will eventually follow behind. But where you ought to spend your time and energy is on the 20%, the early adopters, who will lead the way.

*12. THE PERFORMANCE OF TEACHERS (Appendix K)

I have a unique perspective on this subject. I am a former high school math teacher, married to a college teacher, with two brothers and lots of friends who are current or former teachers. And, partly for these reasons, the teacher bashing that goes on in our society these days makes me pretty angry. Here is a thought experiment that will help clarify some of the issues associated with teacher performance.

Pretend, for a moment, that I can split you into two people and give you two separate teaching assignments for one year. You, Version A, are given a 3rd grade class in an upper middle class neighborhood. You, Version B, are given a 3rd grade class in a poor urban neighborhood. In both cases, your most important job is to teach the children in your class to read. At the end of the year, you will be evaluated on the basis of the average reading scores in your classrooms. The one of you with the higher score will be retained. The one with the lower score will be fired. Which of you will be fired and why?

The answer is obvious. The children in the poorer classroom started out with lower scores and finished with lower scores. You did a lousy job teaching this class. You are a bad teacher and deserve to be fired.

OK. That's not fair. Let's change the rules. Let's look at the amount of improvement in reading from the beginning of the year to the end of the year. Well the one of you who taught in the poor school still gets fired because the children not only started off behind, but more of them have learning difficulties, live in homes where there are no books and have parents who can't read.

So, that's not fair either. You can't compare classes in two different schools like that. Let's back up and give you two different classes in the same school. But you will quickly see that the same thing happens between two classes in the same school. Some students will do better or worse for reasons that have nothing to do with how good you are as a teacher.

Fast forward to the Olympic Diving Competitions. Diver A does a triple back flip off the high dive but misses the water entry. Diver B does a swan dive off the low dive but nails the entry. How can we compare Diver A and Diver B? The Olympic Committee has an answer: "degree of difficulty." One dive is harder than the other and is judged differently.

The same principle could be applied to teaching. But imagine how much harder it would be to assign a "degree of difficulty" to a child. Now try creating a degree of difficulty for a whole class. Now think about how to adjust that degree of difficulty over the year as the class changes when children move in and out of classrooms and schools.

There is a lot of discussion these days about getting rid of "bad teachers." You would think from hearing this that the problems in our education system are caused principally by a large number of bad teachers that the system refuses to fire. One could, of course, make a similar irrational case that the problem with our legal system is a large number of bad lawyers that the system refuses to debar. The problem with our medical system is a large number of bad doctors that the system refuses to decertify. The point is that there are no shortcuts in employee evaluation. There is no simple way to use achievement test data to evaluate teachers, any more than there are simple ways to use patient data to evaluate doctors or court data to evaluate lawyers. Anyone who believes otherwise doesn't know very much about teaching (medicine or law).

This does not mean that we can not use data to improve our education system. Using data to drive school improvement is different than using data to evaluate teachers. When schools make use of data to drive improvement, it is usually site-based (or school level) data, not individual teacher data (e.g. total school 3rd grade reading scores). Such schools have a place where trend data on achievement test scores, attendance rates, graduation rates and rates of teacher retention are prominently displayed. There is an inclusive process for interpreting this data and taking action that involves a wide range of partners, including teachers, principals, superintendents, parents, business leaders, the faith community, elected officials, the media and the students themselves.

When school improvement is managed this way it has a much greater chance of success and is far more constructive than blaming teachers or anyone else. The vast majority of teachers are dedicated hard-working professionals who often work under extremely difficult conditions. People who suggest that fixing schools equates to firing teachers do so because it is easier to name scapegoats than do the hard work of making our schools better.

So how should we evaluate teachers? Individual performance evaluation in education or any other service system should be a byproduct of good supervision that happens throughout the year, not a once-a-year scoring system. (See the essay below on How to do and how not to do individual performance evaluation.) Generally we have done a poor job of teaching people how to be good supervisors. What good supervisors do is set expectations and hold people accountable for meeting those expectations. Performance feedback is done once a week or once a month, not once a year. Keeping records of data along with peer and supervisory observation could allow a construc-tive end of year discussion of strengths and weaknesses. And in those rare cases where someone needs to be fired, the more frequent records have a much better chance of standing up to challenge than achievement test data.

An approach based on annual scoring has none of these benefits, and actually makes things worse by creating resentment and lowering morale. Data can sometimes inform the weekly, monthly and annual supervisory discussions. But the purpose of the data then becomes to help teachers get better at what they do, not judge, punish or fire them. If we really want a better education system, let's concentrate on school im-provement planning. Let's give teachers the support they need, including adequate pay, good supervision and opportunities for professional development. Calculating performance scores for teachers and pretending that they are fair is almost the worst thing we can do. Who is brave enough these days to stand up to the conventional wis-dom and say that the "Emperor of data based teacher evaluation" has no clothes?

See Appendix K for Additional notes on teacher performance evaluation.

*13. WHEN INFRASTRUCTURE IS THE CUSTOMER

The question "Is anyone better off?" works well for programs that directly serve peo-ple. But what if the link to people goes through physical infrastructure? When your job is to build and maintain roads, bridges, water systems, electrical grids, gas distri-bution networks etc. the people served by these systems are better off if the systems themselves work well.

It is sometimes useful to think of the infrastructure itself as a "customer." If a bridge is a "customer" then the condition of the bridge becomes the subject of the "better off" measures.

Roads are the customers of the Department of Transportation, just as much as the peo-ple who ride on them. So % of roads in good condition is an *Is anyone better off?* meas-ure for a Department of Transportation.

Figure 3.3 shows a great example of turning the curve on an infrastructure measure from London, Ontario, Canada. London has a water system that is over 150 years old. They are steadily relining the pipes. And as they do so, the number of water main breaks (the zigzag line) follows a classic Turn the Curve pattern. The line going toward zero is the forecast if the relining program continues. The line going up to the right is the pro-jection if the program stops. This is one of the longest baselines I have seen, almost 70 years. This picture is not about implementing RBA. It is beautiful work that was done before the Water and Sewer Division had ever heard about RBA. It is another example of how Turn the Curve thinking is the natural way that successful people work.

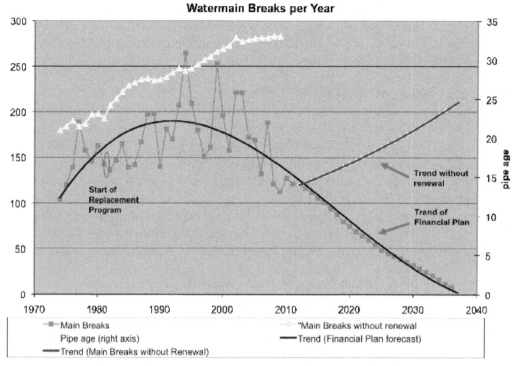

Figure 3.3

*14. HOW TO DO (and how not to do)
INDIVIDUAL EMPLOYEE EVALUATION

Let me be clear. RBA is not designed for individual employee evaluation. It can be used to evaluate team level performance, program, agency and service system level performance, but not individual performance. It must be part of the obsession with testing in our society that we need to give everything and everyone a score. When it comes to employee evaluation we try to tell people how they're doing with a score. And it always does more harm than good.

In 40 years of working with the public and non-profit sectors, I have never seen a good annual employee evaluation process. Mostly what these processes do is make people angry. Think about your own experience. If you don't get straight A's on the evaluation, you're disappointed. Supervisors know this, of course, because they have the same experience with their own evaluations. So there is pressure to give higher scores than might be deserved (they call it "grade inflation" in education) and because it takes a lot of time and energy to defend anything less than perfect scoring. But here's the most important part of all this. Employee scoring does NOTHING to improve employee performance and most often has NEGATIVE effects on employee morale. That's because the very process of doing scored annual evaluations is HOPELESSLY FLAWED.

Instead we need to think about employee evaluation, not as a separate annual function, but as something that is part and parcel of day to day, week to week, and month to month supervision. Good supervisors set high expectations for their employees and hold them to those expectations. This is done in at least two ways: 1) on a day to day basis through "walking around" management, and 2) in weekly or monthly individual one-on-one supervisory meetings. (Supervisors need to be trained in how to do this.) This is the place where constructive feedback can make a difference. It doesn't require much in the way of forms and it certainly doesn't need any kind of score. When I supervised a lot of people many years ago, I kept notes on the things we agreed would be done by the next meeting. I would always ask what they needed from me. And if something wasn't going well, the conversation was not about blame but about how to fix it. In those relatively rare instances where an employee was not performing up to expectations, we could have a candid conversation in a weekly or monthly meeting that could never happen in a single annual evaluation session, for the simple reason that the evidence about performance was fresh and rarely a matter of dispute. And because there is no scoring involved, nothing going on the permanent record, no pay raise at stake, it was possible to have a constructive conversation.

Now if annual scoring evaluations are intrinsically flawed, imagine how much worse they become when you attach financial rewards and punishments. It becomes a BAD PROCESS ON STEROIDS. In government and the nonprofit community, pay increases should be predictable and automatic based on time of service. Period! Pay adjustments are no place to make fine grain distinctions between employees and the quality of their work. (See the entry on why pay for performance has no place in government. See also why you should not use student test scores in teacher evaluation.) And money has been shown time and again to be surprisingly far down on the list of what motivates people to do a good job. More powerful are a sense of accomplishment, recognition, respect, autonomy, and status. In an excellent article titled "Money is not the best motivator," *Forbes Magazine* reported, "The perception of status increases significantly whenever people are given credible informal praise for daily tasks rather than waiting for annual results." (Forbes Magazine, June 2010. Thanks to David Burnby for the citation.)

If you're going to have an annual performance meeting with each employee, make the agenda about what they are going to be doing in the next year, what they hope to accomplish, what you hope to accomplish, and what the organization hopes to accomplish. In this context, you can have a discussion of strengths (start positive) and things they need to work on (traditionally and unhelpfully, called weaknesses).

There will be times when you need to fire someone. It's tough. You need to be clear and strong. I have done it. It's no fun. But the annual evaluation is not such a time. Firing people can be done when necessary in one of two ways: 1) close to the triggering event or 2) after an accumulated written record of inadequate performance gathered on a day by day, week by week basis, exactly the kind of record you will have if you do employee "evaluation" as part of supervision.

These are some of the reasons why current employee appraisal systems have become the monstrosities that they are. It's time for the government and nonprofit sectors to get rid of the charade of annual scored performance evaluations and evaluation-based financial rewards. It's time to use what we know about what really motivates people to help employees and organizations perform at a high level.

PS: It is also not useful to have a four page annual employee "performance plan." I had an argument with an un-named HR director who had put this requirement in place for all the employees of a moderately large local government. Not only did everyone have to develop one of these, but they had to keep it up to date throughout the year. This took a lot of effort and everyone (except the HR director) thought it was a total waste of time. No one was willing to challenge this requirement and my objections made no difference. As far as I know these poor people are still doing this. A one page plan for periodic discussion with your supervisor might be useful. Once again, a simple good idea can become a problem in the hands of overzealous management.

PPS: Here's another idea. Why not ask each employee to keep a daily list of accomplishments. It doesn't have to be detailed or complicated. A simple list. At the end of each day, people could look back on what they were able to get done that day. I do this myself and it helps on days when it feels like nothing has been accomplished. This list could be just for personal use. Or it could be something to be shared and maybe even (carefully) used in supervisory discussions.

15. THE RATIONALE BEHIND THE QUESTION IS *ANYONE BETTER OFF?*

RBA is the only framework (as far as I know) where performance measurement categories are stated in the form of questions. The idea is that plain language questions communicate better than jargon. *How much did we do?* and *How well did we do it?* seem pretty straightforward. But where did *Is anyone better off?* come from? It seems like a pretty harsh way to ask about the effect of our work.

The question was chosen over many other possibilities precisely because it is an unceremonious challenge. And, perhaps more importantly, because it is the voice of the taxpayer. It is the question that SHOULD be asked by the people who fund programs (whether taxpayers, legislators or charities), and by the people who invest energy in programs (whether staff, donors or volunteers). The phrasing is intended to get people's attention and to help shake off the old comfortable answers.

The question explicitly or implicitly incorporates at least four other questions: *Who is better off?; How are they better off?; How did the program contribute?;* and *Is the investment in this program worth it?* Also included is an implied statement about transparency: *We, the people, are watching and will not settle for the old easy answers.* This idea of watching and asking tough questions is at the heart of how accountability works, or how it should work.

It may be tempting to soften the question, to make it more palatable and perhaps more polite. But something is lost when you do that. Embracing *Is anyone better off?* with its sharp edges, signals strength, that we are OK with tough questions, that we are willing to hold ourselves to higher standards, that we are prepared to be accountable.

One more comment. It is important to stay away from categories that imply causality. "How much change did we produce?" is a common and tempting way to formulate effect measures. But, when it comes to improving customers' lives, you simply don't control all the factors that go into such improvements. And pretending that we can know this with any certainty is not the answer. In TH Chapter 4, the section "Is my program working," provides some ways to deal with this, including comparisons of two points in time, and, of course, research and evaluation studies. In the end we should talk about **contribution** to customer well-being. The category "Is anyone better off?" is deliberately silent on the matter of causality.

16. THE WORDING OF THE OTHER TWO RBA PERFORMANCE MEASUREMENT CATEGORIES
(How much did we do? How well did we do it?)

Now that we have *Is anyone better off?* out of the way, what about the other two categories?

The first thing to talk about is the use of the word "we." There were three possible constructions that could have been used: *I, you or we.*

> *How much did I do? and How well did I do it?*
> *How much did YOU do?" How well did YOU do it? and*
> *How much did WE do? How well did WE do it?*

Why is the version with the word "we" so far superior to the other choices?

Let's dispense with "I" first. This perspective is simply too narrow to be broadly applicable to the wide range of programs and agencies around the world. The performance of a program or agency almost always involves more than one person.

But what is wrong with *How much did YOU do?* and *How well did YOU do it??* The problem with this construction comes from the perspective of who is asking the question. In the question *How much did YOU do?* the questioner is in the role of an external agent. It could be a funder, an elected official, a board member, an evaluator, an auditor, a monitor or even a supervisor. This is often how accountability has worked in the past. We collect data to meet the needs of others.

But the most important work of Performance Accountability must be for ourselves. WE must ask OURSELVES about how WE are doing in OUR work. We do this together as colleagues and partners. And this little shift in psychology has profound implications for how the whole process works. The use of the word "we" signifies that we are all in this together and that we are taking ownership of our performance. Such ownership is a pre-condition of any serious effort to improve.

We will of course continue to answer to external authorities. But when we do this work for ourselves first, it is much more likely to be meaningful and useful. So the right questions are, *How much did **we** do?* and *How well did **we** do it?* It is funny how subtleties in the use of words can be so important.

Now let's take on the matter of past tense. Consider these three logical possibilities:

> *How much DID we do?*
> *How much ARE we doing?*
> *How much WILL we do?*

How much are we doing is the present tense. It references things in progress. But data is by definition past tense. Even if it is reporting on something in process, the actual data values must be past tense, even if is the very recent past. So past tense references to data are more universally applicable. Future tense is about targets, goals or expectations and must be addressed separately under those concepts. When it comes to proposing future values, the construction *"How much did we do?* might seem a little awkward. But that awkward phrasing is avoidable in a number of ways. "What is your projection/target/goal for *How much did we do?* measures" works reasonably well. And mostly these conversations are not about the performance measure category itself but about specific measures where it all works perfectly well.

You might think this is much ado about nothing, and maybe it is. But it is also surprising how often these questions come up.

17. IS ANYONE WORSE OFF?

In identifying measures for the "Is anyone better off" category we usually ask "If the service works really well, how are our customers better off?" But the reverse question can sometimes produces important answers. "If the service doesn't work well or work at all, how would our customers be worse off?" These answers can point to important and useful measures. For example, if the child protection service doesn't work well, children will be re-abused. This points to the rate of re-abuse, or more practically, the percentage of children at intake who were previously returned home after an initial finding of confirmed abuse. Another example: the percentage of people completing a remedial driver's education program for DWI offenders with a repeat DWI offense. Remember that these numbers will never be perfect. The point of measurement is not so much about demonstrating achievement as it is about progress, in this case doing better than the baseline forecast over time.

18. IMPLEMENTATION COACHING AND "HOW DO WE…?" QUESTIONS

For those of you who are helping people implement RBA, I have found that the best way to handle implementation coaching sessions is to ask for people to phrase their questions in the form "How do we…….?" For example, "How do we set performance measures for our counseling service?" or "How do we use RBA in our budget process?" or "How do we link our program outcomes to the community's agenda?"

The phrasing implies ownership of the problem. And when people phrase questions in this way, the conversation very quickly gets to the heart of the matter. The "How do we" phrasing makes it more likely that the question concerns something they are actually trying to do, or need to do, or better yet, want to do, as opposed to the endless list of topics we "could or should" talk about. The topic-generated conversation is likely to wander for quite some time before settling down to the part that is of practical concern.

In addition to RBA 101 and Training for Trainers and Coaches, I sometimes conduct a coaching day where we divide the day into a series of one hour sessions. Teams of no more than 10 people come in to discuss their work. I ask that people bring their work products to review, and each person is asked to bring at least one "How do we…?" question. This structure enables us to look at the work to date and engage in a constructive discussion about how to do the work going forward. In some cases we actually do some of the work that has been problematic, such as identifying performance measures for a challenging service.

For those of you who have taken the RBA Training for Trainers and Coaches, this could be a good method to use in organizing your coaching work.

19. DON'T WASTE TIME DEBATING WHETHER A MEASURE IS *How well?* or *Better off?*

You can sometimes get into this debate about whether a measure goes in the *How well did we do it?* quadrant, or the *Is anyone better off?* quadrant. There will be some cases where you could make a case for either placement. Almost any categorization scheme will generate such debates. If you want to see passion about categories, check out the decades long arguments in biological taxonomy.

When this happens, my advice is to just put it somewhere and move on. The UR and LR quadrants will be the starting point for selection of headline performance measures. Both quadrants will be considered. Nothing will be lost with one placement or the other.

The debates about how to interpret a measure can sometimes be interesting and even fun to pursue. They can sometimes be opportunities to learn more about the RBA performance measurement categories. But if the discussion goes on for any length of time, it can slow down the process and be frustrating for other group members.

20. DATA DEVELOPMENT AGENDA CREATIVITY

Remember that RBA ALWAYS starts with existing data. Processes that start with collecting new data are almost certain to get stalled and later abandoned. Waiting for new data is an excuse for inaction.

Working with a friend today on a list of performance measures, and many of them are measures for which they do not currently have data. Naturally this quickly populates the Data Development Agenda (DDA). But there is a concern that the high percentage of DDA measures might be discouraging. "We put so much work into identifying these measures and look how far we still have to go."

I have yet to find a program/service without some place to start. There is also a positive side to having a large Data Development Agenda. If people develop a long list of measures for which they do not have data, it means that they are not being constrained by what is. They are thinking creatively. They are stretching to consider the most important ways of measuring success. This is a sign of a healthy thinking process. Those who confine their thinking only to measures with existing data will almost certainly miss important ways to gauge their progress and tell their story.

As noted elsewhere, it is possible to run the Turn the Curve exercises with estimated data for a measure on your Data Development Agenda. The technique in TH Appendix F explains how to do this. The process for identifying the most important performance measures has the side benefit of identifying the least important measures. Most organizations spend an enormous amount of time collecting data they never use. Take this process as an opportunity to pare away unnecessary data collection and free up the time of your front line staff to do the real work.

21. AVERAGE LENGTH OF STAY

This is a methodological entry I left out of TH because it seemed to be too complex and technical. But there is something important to understand about average length of stay (ALS). For many programs ALS is a powerful measure of how well the program is working. It can be used to measure how long children stay in foster care, how long court cases take to be processed, how long case records stay open, how long recipients receive services from various benefit programs, how long maintenance work orders remain open and many other circumstances.

The development of the following methodology started with the Maryland Unemployment Insurance program during the 1979 recession. This was a time when US Department of Labor programs in Maryland were part of what was then called the Department of Employment and Social Services, later to be The Department of Human Resources. During the 1979 recession, the Labor Statistics Division was struggling with how to forecast the effect of various extended benefit scenarios on the total number of people on unemployment benefits and the associated impact on outlays from the Unemployment Insurance Trust Fund. This was a perfect laboratory for ALS research because the periods of entitlement were fixed and almost all participants stayed for the full length of their benefits.

Here is the formula:

ALS = Total monthly caseload divided by monthly (Entrants or Exits)

If you know two of these variables you can calculate the third.

We were able to forecast the new caseload level for any scenario of extended benefits with considerable accuracy. The ALS in this case was given, the length of benefit. And the number of each entrant cohort was also known. The caseload could be calculated by adjusting the equation to:

Total monthly caseload = ALS times monthly (Entrants or Exits)

Why is any of this important? ALS is a crucial performance measure for foster care and a wide range of other programs. We want children to remain in foster care for as short a time as necessary. Without this formula, the only way to get ALS data is by researching individual case records and creating a composite picture. This is time consuming and expensive. The ALS formula allows you to get this valuable measure quickly using two other measures that are routinely reported.

ALS data is an important starting point for the Turn the Curve process. The beauty of this formula is that it gives you ALS data EVERY MONTH. The caseload is known and the number of exits can usually be obtained without much trouble. When data is this current, the RBA Turn the Curve process can be very robust.

Here's another quick example of where we used this. We were responsible for the Child Support Enforcement Program. This is an important program and it generally does a great job. But we discovered that there was an unexpectedly large number of open cases in Baltimore City, and this was complicating workload and staffing calculations. Looking at the total caseload and the number of closed cases each month, we were able to calculate the average time a case record stayed open (ALS) was 29 years! This was conclusive evidence that the caseload size was caused, at least in part, by failure to close cases when supported children reached age 18.

22. HOW TO MEASURE ALIGNMENT (Appendix L)

This is another technical piece. It allows you to calculate the degree of alignment between any two (or more) percentage distributions. I first developed this many years ago to help measure the extent to which the race/ethnicity distribution of foundation staff were aligned with the race/ethnicity distribution of the communities in which they worked. But it has much broader applicability.

One comparison that I experimented with but never finished was the comparison of the race/ethnicity distribution of the US Congress to the US population. Since I had multi-year data for both, I was able to determine that the alignment was steadily declining. Other applications allow a calculation of equity distributions such as the disproportionate representation of minority children in the foster care and juvenile justice systems.

Appendix L shows the details of the calculation methodology. It is set up to produce scores from 0 to 100, but could be adjusted to produce scores in any range. The difficulty with 0-100 scaling is our experience in the education system, where 90+ is an A, and less than 70 is failing. This interpretation is not applicable to these alignment scores, where 70 percent alignment might be very good, depending on the circumstances.

Technical note: When comparing more than two distributions (say race/ethnicity and gender) the divisor of the difference score is increased in proportion to the number of percentage distributions being compared.

23. IT'S OK TO WORK ON SECONDARY MEASURES

We spend a lot of time in RBA focusing on the 3 to 5 Headline Measures for a program/service or a population result/outcome. Headline measures must be ones for which we have good data, so we can get started turning curves. If this process is done well, two other lists are also created: Secondary Measures, for which we have good data, that didn't make the cut as headline measures. And a Data Development Agenda of where we need new or better data.

People sometimes interpret this three part sorting to mean that you shouldn't ever work on measures in the second and third category. But that's not right. If you want to work on turning the curve on a secondary measure, go for it. And you can work on a DDA measure even when you have NO data at all. You can create working baselines based on group consensus (see "Creating baselines from group knowledge" in TH Appendix F)

The point is this. Setting priorities in measurement is important. But those priorities should not be taken as a straight jacket. If a particular indicator doesn't make the top 5, there may still be a need to work on it.

24. QUALITATIVE VS. QUANTITATIVE MEASURES CONFUSION

Perhaps you have encountered this question. People get confused by the distinction between quantitative and qualitative measures. They sometimes think that a qualitative measure can't involve data, because it would then be a quantitative measure. Are you following this?

I recently reviewed a provider report submitted to an NSW government agency. The agency disallowed all the percentage measures of quality because "A percentage performance measure, by its very nature, can only be obtained by reference to <u>quantitative</u> data!" This is wrong because it is too-literal an interpretation of the word "quantitative." (Unfortunately, it was allowed to stand as a critique of the provider's report.)

Qualitative measures are of course made up of data. That's what measures are, DATA!

And, yes, data can be used to measure quality. The percentage of people in a drug treat-

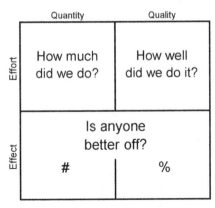

Performance Measurement Categories

Figure 3.4

ment program who get off of drugs is a measure of the quality of that service. The percentage of people in a job training program who get and keep good paying jobs is a measure of the quality of the job training service. If you must use the distinction between quantitative and qualitative measures, then think of it this way: "quantitative measures" are "How much?" measures and "qualitative measures" are "How well?" measures. All the Upper right (UR) and Lower right (LR) quadrant measures are measures of quality. These measures are always rates, ratios or percentages (anything with a numerator and denominator). And yes, they are all made up of, what else, "quantitative" data.

25. MINIMALLY INTRUSIVE DATA COLLECTION

There is a range of services where the choices of Better off? measures are seriously limited by the lack of data based on observable events (e.g. got a job, graduated high school, re-admitted to hospital etc.) Recently, I have had a chance to meet with experts in counseling services, homeless services, and early care and education, where the question of reliable data is a special challenge. In many cases there are not observable improvements that can be tracked and reported. The information must come from client and/or worker observation. What is the right thing to do?

Let's go back to first principles. Data collection is not more important than service delivery. If data collection methods interfere with service delivery they must be changed or abandoned.

Here are some solutions to consider:

- Use data collection instruments that HELP the worker deliver the service.
- Collect data on a sample basis.
- Stop asking clients to fill out assessment forms. Have the worker do the assessment as part of the normal interaction with the client and fill out the questionnaire after the client leaves.
- Generate data from entries already present in case records and avoid using additional worker time.

One problematic line of argument has been that we should use only validated instruments in such services. But the available instruments were developed for research purposes and are often too long, complex and time consuming. And they can be intimidating to clients.

The most important principle in answering these questions is this: What kind of tools are actually useful in the delivery of the service? Forget about data collection for a minute. What would be helpful to the worker and the client? If we can answer this question, it is likely that the data gathered will be meaningful in considering the performance of the service and therefore more meaningful to managers and funders.

26. HOW DO THE 7 QUESTIONS TRANSLATE INTO REPORT FORMATS?

The 7 Question (Leaking Roof, Turn the Curve) thinking process is designed to get you from talk to action. But not all of the 7 questions necessarily show up in the reporting format you use.

Let's take Performance Accountability as our example. (You will easily see that the same approach applies to Population Accountability.) The performance report format would have the following sections:

1. Name of program or service, purpose and contribution to quality of life
2. Baseline graphs (from Question 4: *How are we doing on the most important of these measures?*)
3. Story behind the baselines (also from Question 4 *How are we doing on the most important of these measures?*)
4. Partners who are helping (Question 5. *Who are the partners that have a role to play in doing better?*)
5. Action plan (from Question *7 What do we propose to do?*)

Notice how questions 1 to 3 (*Who are our customers? How can we measure if our customers are better off? How can we measure if we are delivering service well?*) do not show as sections of the report. These questions are used to identify the most important measures for which baselines are prepared. Keeping a list of CUSTOMERS is a good idea. Having a separate record of the four quadrant work leading to your selection of headline measures and the Data Development Agenda is also a good idea, and these documents can be updated from time to time.

Question 5 *Who are the partners with a role to play in doing better?* and *What works to do better?* don't usually show up in the report format. Be careful when it comes to publicly listing partners. Use the partners list and their potential roles to shape your recruitment process, and then use it to guide your private conversation with each partner. Only when a partner has actually taken action to help Turn the Curves, and is comfortable with the visibility of that role, should you list them on a performance report.

Question 6 *What works to do better, including no-cost/low-cost ideas?* is an "off line" discussion. This should produce a shopping list, from which your Question 7 action plan is drawn. It can sometimes be useful to show the thinking behind question 6 in an appendix, so that you have a record of your thinking about best and promising practice and potential actions (and *What would it take?*).

Notice how this description of a performance report compares favorably to the Welsh Epilepsy report discussed above and the Wyoming Part II report in TH Chapter 6.

*27. RBA on RBA: USING RBA TO TRACK RBA IMPLEMENTATION IN ANGLICARE WESTERN AUSTRALIA

by Desiree Nangle with thanks to Ian Carter, Executive Director, and Anglicare WA staff (Appendix M)

Anglicare WA has been on a journey of building a culture of evaluation and continuous improvement across the organisation. Our organisation began implementing RBA at an agency wide level in 2011 following a successful two year pilot project that led to continued funding in our Youth service area. Since then we have expanded the use to cover nearly all (91%) of Anglicare WA's 68 programs across the state as well as in corporate services such as Occupational Health and Safety, Human Resources, and our annual Christmas Giving Operations. We have seen concrete benefits from using RBA including 1) service staff and teams taking time to reflect on practice and outcomes, 2) evidence based decisions being made as a result of RBA data analysis, and 3) improved outcomes for our clients!

While the main objective of this outcomes measuring initiative has been to build a culture of evaluation allowing for continuous service improvement for our clients, it is added benefit if service staff support it and find it useful. This thinking led to our meta-evaluation (RBA on RBA) that has been collected alongside services' RBA frameworks since 2011.

Our work on RBAing RBA has benefited the agency by giving us a snapshot of general attitudes and opinions towards the framework as well as identifying common barriers and opportunities RBA has presented to service areas and staff. This has allowed our Research and Evaluation team to focus in on any issues and adjust our RBA training and vision to allow for staff experiences of the framework in day-to-day work. This work additionally evidenced the benefit seen in RBA from an across agency perspective. These results, along with lived experience and witnessed benefits, allowed Anglicare WA to confidently commit to continuing on our RBA journey for the foreseeable future.

[Appendix M shows three charts from Anglicare WA] The first shows performance measures used to track implementation of RBA. The second shows a theoretical framework for "Phases of RBA Implementation." And the third is a report on RBA implementation modeled after the Welsh Epilepsy Unit report discussed above.

This is the most advanced effort I know of to track RBA implementation in a large organization. Desiree's advice: "The most important thing to track and measure is the extent of actual use of RBA and the % who see RBA as useful."

These tools can be used with the RBA Implementation Self Assessment Questionnaire (Appendix G). Appendix M also shows some additional RBA Implementation questions to consider in shaping future research.

CHAPTER 4:
Choosing Performance Measures for Selected Services

In this section we address how to choose performance measures for types of services that pose special challenges.

*1. HOW TO MEASURE "CAPACITY BUILDING"

People want to "build capacity" in organizations, in communities, in partnerships, etc. But capacity building can be such a vague purpose. What does it really mean? And how could you know if you were making progress? It turns out that "capacity building" can be CLEARLY ARTICULATED AND MEASURED using a technique discussed in TH Chapter 7 Composite Measures.

First list all the capacities you are interested in building. This might include things such as governance, leadership, performance management, citizen engagement, fund raising etc. Then narrow this list down to the top ten. For each capacity, get your group together and rate how you are currently doing on a scale of 1 to 5. Then go back and add up the number of capacities on which you rated 4 or 5. Let's say it's 6 of the 10. Create a baseline graph like the one below. Plot the score "6" in the middle of the x axis. Then estimate where you think you've been in the last few years (backcasting). Have things been getting better, worse or about the same? Let's say things have been getting slightly better. The consensus is that it was more likely 5 a few years ago. Then you can do the forecast. Where do you think you'll be in a few years if you don't do anything more or different than what you're doing now? (Note this is not where you WANT to go, but rather where you are going if you don't do something more or different.) Let's say your consensus forecast is that you'll stay at 6 unless you do something more or different.

You now have a curve to turn, and the full Turn the Curve thinking process can be brought to bear. What's the *story behind the curve*? Who are the partners who have a role to play in doing better? *What works* to do better? And what do you propose to do? This will get you an action plan and you can get started.

Notice that with this way of constructing the baseline, the story practically tells itself. If you are doing well on 6 capacities, then the other four are obviously where the problems lie and where you need to focus your efforts.

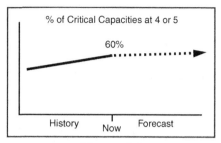

Figure 4.1

The process of rating yourself on these 10 items is, of course, a process of SELF ASSESSMENT. Self assessments are valuable instruments for a number of reasons. They spell out exactly what it means to do well, so that everyone can understand what is expected. And just as importantly they can be done "privately" without worry about the judgments of an external agency, public embarrassment or punishment. This can provide the space needed to take action to get better. Self assessment processes deserve much more widespread use. Check out the RBA/OBA self assessment questionnaire in Appendix G.

With a self assessment process, there is great value in spending time exploring exactly what it means to do well on each capacity. For example, what would it look like if you were doing well on governance? Spell it out. Fashion it into a set of CRITERIA. For example, we would be doing well on governance if we have a representative group, and a common language, where everyone feels they have a voice, where there is transparent decision making, with room for dissent, where action is taken and regularly assessed etc. The more specific you can be, the better. These criteria then become guides to what is required to achieve a high score on each element. This will aid in building consensus on the current score and the actions that need to be taken.

Now some will argue that the "scoring" part of self assessment is imprecise and unscientific. Yes, that's right. You're going to have to use your best facilitation skills to create a group consensus on what a fair score is for each item. And where you end up with disagreement, you might end up with scores in a range, e.g. 2-3. That's OK. As long as everyone defends their score in terms of the established criteria, you will have a healthy and constructive discussion.

This same process can be used to address other difficult but vaguely defined challenges. What is a "thriving neighborhood?" What is a "developed country?" What is a "family-friendly" service? When my kids were little and we were looking for a new house, we did something similar. We helped the kids make a list of all the characteristics they wanted in a new house. We used this to judge how each candidate house stood up to their criteria. This made them feel part of the process, eased the trauma of moving, and ultimately produced a better choice. My favorite criteria was "no ghosts."

*2. PERFORMANCE MEASURES FOR EMPLOYEE MORALE AND RECOMMENDED MORALE SURVEY QUESTIONS

I know of at least one organization that spent more that $100,000 on an employee morale survey, including a fine grained analysis of morale by unit. The questionnaire was quite detailed, so that the exact nature of the complaints could often be determined. If you have this kind of money to throw around, good for you. But it is not necessary.

Instead it is possible to conduct your own morale survey using a simple set of four questions. If you have research and evaluation staff, this is a perfect job for them. If not you may need some help in administering the survey so that it is confidential. But most organizations should be able to read and interpret the findings. This becomes the *story behind the curve* and sets up discussion of actions you can take to get better. The other advantage of do-it-yourself employee morale surveys is that you can afford to do them every year and track progress over time.

The first two questions are rated using a Likert scale.

"Is this a good place to work?" and
"Do you get the support you need to do a good job?"

I believe these questions cover the most important aspects of employee morale. Just as in customer satisfaction surveys, they should be followed by two open-ended questions: "Why did you rate us this way? and "How could we do better?"

Here is some of the reasoning behind these questions. "Good place to work" is a simple but powerful summary of the respondents' attitude toward their work and also their view of the conditions of the workplace. Each person defines "good place" in their own way. But that's OK. It allows different definitions to coexist. "Support I need to do a good job" allows you to zero in on the quality of supervision, support and workload. Problems in these areas are among the most common causes of low morale. The answers to the two open ended questions are gold. You should take these seriously and let them inform your action plan.

It is obviously possible to make this more complicated. My suggestion is try this simpler approach and see if you actually do something with the data. If so, you will stand apart from most organizations where lip service is given to employee morale and reports on the subject languish on the shelf.

*3. THE PERFORMANCE OF ADMINISTRATIVE SERVICES: CONTROL VS. ENABLING

There was a time in my career when I supervised all the internal administrative functions of a large government agency. In the course of this work I came to the realization that all administrative service jobs (human resources, budget and finance, audit, building services, grants management, information technology, etc.) have two different kinds of functions: control and enabling. Often people in administrative jobs are very good at the control function but not so good at the enabling function. Good managers of administrative services must help their staff view other staff in the agency as customers and develop the right balance between control obligations and customer service.

Most performance measures for administrative units address only the control functions, mostly upper right quadrant measures about accuracy and timeliness. But customer satisfaction surveys can tell if the enabling function is being performed well. The customers for administrative services are sometimes all staff of the agency and sometimes primarily the management / supervisory staff. To test the enabling function, the most important question to ask on an administrative services customer satisfaction survey is "Are we providing the support you need to do a good job?" As with the morale survey, you need two more open ended questions: "Why did you rate us this way?" and "How could we do better?"

In one place, they took administrative customer satisfaction seriously. All the administrative units sent out separate surveys at different times. The organization's managers reported that they were "constantly getting surveys." The process quickly deteriorated as over-worked managers saw this as an imposition. The result was low response rates and unreliable data. A better approach is to do this kind of survey once a year. List all the administrative services down the left side of a scoring sheet. Ask the respondent to rate each unit using the method above. This once a year survey has a much better chance of being taken seriously and producing useful findings.

One other point worth mentioning. It is not uncommon to find tension (and sometimes outright warfare) between administrative staff and direct service staff in large organizations. Customer satisfaction surveys can be a bridge that can help improve these relationships. This means taking the findings seriously and acting on suggested changes. The process should have some visibility in the organization's culture. And there should be some form of recognition for good administrative customer service.

4. PERFORMANCE MEASURES FOR ARTS ORGANIZATIONS

What does it mean for customers of arts organizations to be better off? Over the years I've had a chance to work with people who run museums, theaters, artists collectives and other arts organizations. Libraries also fall roughly into this category. There are two measures that consistently come out of these conversations.

First, the number and percentage of repeat visitors. If people come back, they must have gotten something meaningful from their previous visit(s). And, second, interview questions that get at customer satisfaction.

This is where you can be creative. You want to fashion one question that you can ask quickly for some sample of people (e.g. every 10th person) leaving the facility. The way to think about this question is to imagine you are standing in front of your funders, and you get to say "X percent of people exiting the museum/concert hall/gallery said....." What do you think would be most meaningful end to that sentence? Some examples,

> "Did you enjoy your visit today?" or
> "Did you learn anything from your visit today?"

If you have time and can engage in longer conversations with a subset of people, you can begin to dig into the *story behind the curve* and *what works* ideas.

> "What did you find most interesting?" or
> "What did you learn?" or
> "How could we make the (museum) better?"

You can also get demographic data on customers which also helps with the story behind the data and can inform your thinking about actions. It is very important in these longer conversations to be very gracious and thank people taking their time to do this. Once the organization sees that this kind of data is useful (another important test), then the rest of the Turn the Curve thinking process will flow more or less naturally.

Two other things to think about. There is research to be found on the web about the economic value of the arts for communities. Communities with an active arts sector are draws for both visitors and businesses. You can calculate your share of such benefits, by considering the relative size of your organization in the arts sector, and combining research findings with local economic data. Your "economic value" can be used as a *Better off?* measure, one that clearly shows contribution to population quality of life.

Arts organizations can apply the RBA Turn the Curve exercise to fund raising. Here is a curve every organization needs to turn. And RBA can help generate new ideas. Creativity in fund raising is a survival skill for all underfunded organizations.

Finally, a personal note: Baltimore has some of the oldest and best community theaters. I had the good fortune to be given roles in many of these theater productions over the span of 20 years. I have, from this, some personal knowledge of performance art and other art forms. What does it mean for the customers of an arts organization to be 'better off'? This is a serious question worth exploring in its own right. It is certain that the benefits will vary from person to person. Everything from the relief of humor, to the re-imagination of self, to feelings that can barely be articulated let alone

Arts Performance Insights from Vermont

with thanks to Hillary Boone (Benchmarks for a Better Vermont at Marlboro College) and Judy Chalmer (VSA Vermont)

It is possible to measure clear "better offs" for arts programs designed to use arts as a therapeutic tool, or with the purpose of helping people. For example, returning soldiers exposed to the arts may report an increased ability to talk about their experiences or trauma.

A great example of using the arts as a tool to achieve "better off" customer results is VSA Vermont. VSA VT is a statewide nonprofit devoted to using "the magic of the arts to engage the capabilities and enhance the confidence of children and adults with disabilities." The staff has worked together to integrate performance measures throughout their organization, using the turn the curve exercise to ask hard questions and make real changes in how they deliver services. They look for sustained changes in the capabilities and the confidence of their clients, and when things aren't working they adjust their strategies.

VSA Vermont's Start With The Arts (SWTA) early literacy program provides an arts instructor to 36 child care sites and 6 center-based sites each year, representing every county in Vermont. Some of their "better off" measures are listed below, and a full RBA report can be found at vsavt.org.

- #/% childcare providers created, delivered and documented their own 16-week arts-based literacy curriculum over a four-month period

- #/% childcare providers use SWTA credits to gain points in Vermont State's childcare quality Rating System (STARS)

- #/% childcare providers use SWTA PD hours for Advanced Specialized Care status

- #/% children measured in pre and post observations improved in VT Early Learning Standards in: Language Development, Early Reading and Creative Expression

Executive Director Judy Chalmer says, " I love that I work for an organization that is deeply committed to performance measurement, and also has 'magic' in its mission statement." When we work with arts organizations at Benchmarks for a Better Vermont, we are always sure to begin with a conversation about what the organization is hoping to achieve. Although a small nonprofit may not be able to measure the intrinsic value of the arts in a given community, we have found that proxy measures often exist. The arts are a crucial, and a necessary component of human life. It is our challenge and responsibility to work creatively to identify the aspects of quality of life that the arts uphold and restore, and to develop performance measures accordingly.

counted. This is a broad and complex field of effects. So why are we trying to count things? It is quite common for arts organizations to be resistant to both the identification and use of performance measures for a whole range of important philosophical and artistic reasons. It is important to remember that performance measures are **always** a matter of approximation and compromise. Measures like "repeat visits" and customer satisfaction are simply accessible stand-ins for this complex field of effects. It can help arts organizations decide how to improve over time. It can make them more business-like (in a good way). And it can help them make the case for funding. It does not degrade or demean the subtleties of the art itself. And these deeper more powerful effects can be captured in interviews if you are careful about how you record and report them. Finally, think about asking the artists and musicians to draw, paint or compose a piece entitled "Performance Measurement." (For reference see *Guernica* and the Egmont Overture.)

5. PERFORMANCE MEASURES FOR SPACIAL PLANNING/DEVELOPMENT

Spatial planning or Land use planning almost always involves strategies that will affect population quality of life results such as "A Clean and Sustainable Environment," or "Prosperous Economy." For each of these population results, you could establish powerful indicators to which Spatial development / Land use planning contributes.

To come up with performance measures for the planning process itself, you would need to identify the direct and indirect customers of the process (e.g. participants in community engagement process, businesses, residents and people who will read and approve the plan.) Consider each of the specific actions that make up the planning process itself. The 5 Step method in TH Appendix G should yield the usual three to five headline measures.

As a shortcut, a good list of LR measures can be obtained by asking, "What would a good plan and planning process look like?" "What are the characteristics of a good plan and planning process?" "How does our current process rate on each of these characteristics? This can be judged by the planning group itself (via objective criteria and self assessment) and/or a survey of stakeholders and process participants. Such a rating can be treated as a curve to turn. (see the Chapter 2 essay: A shortcut method for choosing population indicators).

I argue in RBA training that strategic planning is a continuous process, never static, always changing. But spatial (land use) planning processes are the exception to this rule. There is a fixed amount of land. A decision to use a parcel of land in one way is a decision against another type of use. Such decisions, once made, are not easily changed. So the stakes are higher and the intensity of controversy is likely to be higher as well. All this means that the concept of "role" becomes even more important. Each decision should be tested to see which alternative choice makes the greater contribution to community quality of life. This kind of debate becomes somewhat easier when quality of life has been first articulated in the form of population results. It helps if people agree on these conditions in advance of the planning process. Then, when people argue about the matter of role and contribution to quality of life, at least they are arguing about the right things.

One more thing: Remember that "Sustainable Development" is actually not a population result or outcome (although it is now often being treated that way). It is a means and not an end in itself. Development is most often used to signify a type of action in support of true end conditions like a sustainable environment, sustainable culture or sustainable economy.

6. PERFORMANCE MEASURES FOR INFORMATION AND REFERRAL AND FOLLOWUP TO SERVICES

There are three progressively more important lower right measures:

1) % of referred clients who connect to the referred service,
2) % of referred clients who receive help from the referred service and
3) % of clients who are better off in some way as a consequence of receiving those services.

All of these measures are difficult to get and require some kind of structured follow-up contact with the client and/or the referred service. For information and referral service, this follow-up can and should be conceived of as a part of the service itself. If this followup is not possible for all customers, then the service should ask (say every 5th or 10th caller) if it is OK to call back in a week to see how they're doing.

One I&R service made the mistake of assigning these follow-up calls to inexperienced new staff, who were calling principally for the purpose of data collection. These follow-up calls should, instead, be made by the most experienced staff, who now have a second chance to help the customer if help is still needed. Data collection is, and always should be, a byproduct of doing the real work.

The techniques used for information and referral have applicability to all services where followup information about customer status is important. It is often difficult to locate and contact customers after they have left a service. This means that contacting customers soon after leaving (e.g. one week vs. 6 months) is more likely to be successful. I recently learned of a service where Google donated phones for clients to take with them. The clients received credits if they called in on some regular basis. After one year, they owned the phone and could take over paying for continuing service. For programs serving the homeless, provision of a phone can be life changing help, enabling people to have a contact number for job applications, health appointments etc. Basic cell/mobile phone service these days is cheap and the ability to be connected in this way will eventually be considered a human right. Consider making it part of the package of services that you deliver to vulnerable and socially isolated customers.

7. PERFORMANCE MEASURES FOR VOLUNTEERS AND VOLUNTEERISM

The overall rate of volunteering (% of adults and young people who volunteer in a given year) is a common measure of civic engagement and can serve as a population indicator for a result like "Engaged Community." This in turn can produce a baseline curve to turn at the community level. The volunteer rate for the United States, as measured by the federal Bureau of Labor Statistics, was 26.8% for the year ending September 2011[19]. "The State of Volunteering in Australia (2012)," cites ABS data showing 36% of the adult population in Australia volunteered in 2010[20]. These reports are full of useful ideas about policy and are worth studying. See the citations below.

With regard to performance measures, there are a wide range of *How well* and *Better off* measures that could be used, having to do with the organizations that sponsor volunteers and volunteers themselves. Here are some measures to consider:

- % of organizations in a given network making use of volunteers.
- Volunteer hours (or dollar equivalent) as a percentage of total organizational hours (or total budget).
- % of volunteers who are first time volunteers.
- % of volunteers who are repeat volunteers.
- % of volunteers who say they have been treated well.
- % of volunteers to report they feel they have made a difference.

Heather Hewitt commented on the RBA Facebook posting of these ideas: "As part of the success of building community capacity I would measure
- #/% of volunteers who go on to gain employment
- % volunteers who gain confidence in themselves, in looking for work, or taking on more responsibility within the volunteer program
- % who are satisfied with the level of training
- % who receive constructive (or any) feedback
- % of volunteers who use the skills they gain in volunteering work to help with other work or their personal life."

---

[19] www.bls.gov/news.release/volun.nr0.htm
[20] www.volunteeringaustralia.org/files/YTRRXXK3TQ/VA_State_of_Volunteering_in_ Australia_2012_screen_FINAL.pdf

8. PERFORMANCE MEASURES FOR ADVOCACY

Many organizations have some form of advocacy (UK, "campaigning") as part of the organization's mission or purpose. In these cases, the organization should have some form of an advocacy agenda. Such agendas typically include recommended changes in law, policies and allocation of resources, directed at elected officials or the leaders of important social institutions.

In other words, the organization wants certain people to do certain things. This lays the groundwork for *Is anyone better off?* performance measures. What percentage of the advocacy agenda is actually adopted? More generally, what percentage of the people you want to do something actually do it? (i.e. changing policies, passing laws, increasing budgets). A simple example: We had 10 items on our legislative agenda and three of them passed.

Here's a harder example. A charitable foundation advocates for county level policy changes in education, health, child welfare and juvenile justice. There are 3,000 counties in the United States. What percentage of those 3,000 counties have actually adopted any of the recommended policies? Since counties are not of equal size, what is the population-weighted percentage of adoption?

Often the LL version of these performance measures shows up in the annual narrative report of accomplishments. "Four counties adopted our policy last year." What is not usually published is that four counties is just a little more than one tenth of one percent of 3,000 counties (LR). This is not a criticism of the advocacy organization or its annual report. You expect people to frame accomplishments this way in reports to the board and the public. The problem arises when this measurement of proportion is absent from the private internal discussions, when the percentage of all counties is not a chart on the wall, when this bigger picture measure is not even considered. The risk is that we become satisfied with low levels of success. If we are serious about this work, if we really believe that what we are proposing is dramatically better than current policy or practice, we should not settle for small successes. Certainly celebrate each and every one. But put the chart on the wall, talk about the big ambitions, the "What would it take?" question, and struggle against "small success" becoming good enough.

The spread of RBA is a perfect example of this. I advocate for the adoption of a certain set of ideas. I estimate that the RBA/OBA worldwide practitioner community currently exceeds 100,000 people. Sounds pretty good, right? But, counting the US and countries where English is the first language, I estimate that there are more than 40 million people in government and nonprofit jobs, and likely many more, who could benefit from RBA. 100,000 is less than three tenths of one percent of 40 million. This number gets much smaller when all countries are considered. This creates the constant struggle against the temptation to consider the significant growth in RBA as good enough.

The true ambition is for RBA to become the world standard for how people work together to improve quality of life and how organizations plan, budget and manage their services. This is not megalomania. (Psychologists feel free to weigh in.) It is the simple belief that RBA is better than the alternatives. There is a long way to go.

9. PERFORMANCE MEASURES FOR PARTNERSHIPS

There are many different types of partnerships in the world today, working at every level from communities to counties, states, nations and the global community. How do you measure the performance of this type of entity?

The first thing to understand is that partnerships are almost always concerned with population level or service system level improvements. This means that the distinction between Population Accountability and Performance Accountability is more important than ever. If the partnership is concerned with population quality of life, it must be clear about which population results and indicators it is trying to influence. If the partnership is concerned with improvements to a service system, it must be clear about which service system performance measures it is trying to improve. If the partnership is working on both population and performance it must be able to see its work on service system improvements as a means to the ends of population change. Many partnerships lack this clarity.

Consider, for example, a Health Planning Board. The Board must see that it is working to improve the health care service system (reduced use of emergency rooms/departments and increased investment in preventive care etc.) as a contribution to improving population indicators (e.g. rates of cancer, heart disease, diabetes etc.) associated with the population result "Healthy People." A Safeguarding Children Board must be able to see its work on improving the child and family service system (e.g. increasing investment in family support services, improved response time to reports of child abuse etc.) as contributing to the improvement of population indicators associated with "Safe Children" (e.g. the population incidence and prevalence of child abuse, child neglect and domestic violence etc.).

Partnerships need to know when they are having a population conversation and when they are having a service system performance conversation. The reason is quite simple and is easily illustrated by a real example (without name). A state partnership was convened with foundation support under the rubric of child and family "service system reform." A lot of terrific work was done inside government agencies and with NGO partners. But the very naming and construction of the work suggested that fixing the service system was the principle purpose of the work. This is not the same thing as improving the quality of life of children and families in the community. Improving service system performance is important work. But service system performance could be dramatically improved while the population conditions we care about get worse. This is because fixing the service system is just one part of what must be a larger strategy to improve the quality of life of all children and families. Many health care boards focus so intently on improving the health care delivery system that they fail to see the importance of working with people and organizations outside the health system to take on actual population health conditions. Fixing the service system is not the same thing as fixing quality of life.

The challenge of being clear about this distinction is complicated in those cases where a service system performance measure doubles as a population indicator. This happens most often in the education system. The high school graduation rate or the percent of students with five good GCSE's are performance measures for the school system. But they are ALSO commonly used as indicators of population quality of life conditions such as "All children grow up to be happy, productive contributing adults." **This means that the work of improving education service system measures can be conceived of in two different ways**. It can be seen as the sole responsibility of the Board of Education. The Board may reach out to community partners, though this is relatively rare. Any service system is prone to think it should be able to fix things without "outside" involvement. The alternative is to conceive the work as a matter of community partnership where leaders from the education community work alongside the many other partner in the community who have something to contribute to school success. If voters, tax payers and elected officials see school success narrowly as the "job" of the Board of Education, they are more likely to blame the board when rates don't improve. In healthy community partnerships, blame is more rare, because it is not useful in turning curves.

Having said all that, the matter of measuring the performance of the partnership itself is not often undertaken. Partnerships regularly track population indicators and service system performance measures (whether they know the difference or not). But how good is the partnership itself?

There are some *How much did we do?* measures that are generic to this type of organization, that we can quickly dispense with, including: # of partners, # of meetings, # of reports, # of events etc.

Here are some important *How well did we do it?* measures to consider:

> % of all (people, organizations) who **should** be in the partnership who **are** in the partnership and who are **active** members.. This requires that the partnership first develop a list of potential partners. This is a useful activity in its own right. It allows Turn the curve thinking to be applied to the percent who are active, and this in turn can lead to action plans for engagement and recruitment.

% partners who think the partnership is well-run and the meetings are useful

% of partnership meeting participants who are decision makers

For partnerships with an active funded agenda or program:
- % of funds by source
- Ratio of total funds to initial investment funds. This is sometimes known as "leverage" and can be used to help identify the extent to which the partnership is generating contributions from new funders.

Is anyone better off? measures depend on the purpose of the partnership. A partnership working at the population quality-of-life level should articulate its purposes in terms of population results and indicators. This then enables the partnership to judge its progress in terms of:

% of indicator curves with a robust turn the curve strategy in place.
% of indicator curves headed in the right direction.
% of indicator curves that have turned.

Notice this is a little trick that allows population indicators to be morphed into performance measures for the organization trying to change them. There is a danger here that this will confuse Population and Performance Accountability and you have to decide if it is worth the risk. Population Accountability will always be bigger than any partnership no matter how broadly constructed. And population indicator curves should always be separately displayed in conference room charts on the wall, and public presentations and reports. See the reporting formats in TH Chapter 6 that clearly separate population and performance elements.

For partnerships working on improving a service system (e.g. health care services, child welfare services, etc.) *Is anyone better off?* measures will have to do with the extent to which the service system UR and LR performance measures have improved. For example, a collaborative working to improve the health care service system might look at:

UR: Rate of use of emergency rooms (vs. preventive care)
UR: Waiting times and waiting lists
LR: Rate of repeat hospital admissions for the same illness

Remember that the other two ways of measuring progress (accomplishments and stories) will figure prominently in reporting on progress, in addition to data.

If you have found this discussion challenging, remember that the boundary between service system performance and population well-being is the most complex part of RBA. In Chaos and Complexity Theory we would call this a "turbulent boundary." So it takes a little extra effort to figure things out in this space.

CHAPTER 5:
Putting Population and Performance Together
(and stuff that didn't quite fit anywhere else)

*1. THE RELATIONSHIP BETWEEN PROGRAMS AND POPULATION RESULTS

It is embedded in the very nature of Population and Performance Accountability that 1) Any given program will contribute to more than one population result and 2) any given population result will require contributions from more than one program.

This non-linear relationship between Population and Performance Accountability is a truth about the way the world works, and not something we can choose to accept or not.

The most common problem occurs when people want to write a report on "Prosperous Economy" and list all the programs that contribute to "Prosperous Economy." Almost any list of programs contributing to "Prosperous Economy" will also contribute to other population results. Job training, for example, also contributes to "Strong Families" and "Safe Communities." Is it OK to put job training in more than one place? In traditional rollup accounting, a given program goes in one and only one place. To do otherwise creates the accounting sin of double counting.

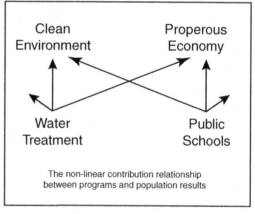

The non-linear contribution relationship between programs and population results

Figure 5.1

The truth is that, when showing the relationship between Population and Performance Accountability, rollup rules no longer apply. They work fine inside the bureaucracy and Performance Accountability. Programs roll up to divisions which roll up to agencies. But in crossing the line from performance to population, the rollup paradigm doesn't work. This is one of the most important insights in RBA and explains why so many previous attempts to cleanly link each program to one population result have failed.

If this is not clear, consider another example closer to home. List all the people (family and friends) who have helped you succeed in graduating from high school. Now list all the people who have helped you get a job. Now list all the people who have helped you stay healthy. There will be a lot of overlap between these lists, right? "Graduating from school," "Getting a Job" "Staying Healthy" might be considered your personal "results or outcomes" Each person, in this example, is a program that contributes to more than one result. Each result requires more than one contributor.

Sometimes, people try to reduce this complex set of program-to-result relationships to a simple one-to-one correspondence. This was done in the case of a budget in an unnamed state, where the state assigned a unique four digit identifier to each program in state government. The Division of Water Quality was given a number that clearly and cleanly rolled up into the Department of the Environment. No problem here. But the four digit number also rolled the Water Quality Division up to the single population result "Clean Environment." Certainly, Water quality contributes to a clean environment. But it also contributes to many other quality of life results as well. These other relationships were lost, or more likely misunderstood and ignored.

When it is absolutely necessary to have an unduplicated count, this paring down to a single relationship can be used to assign programs and their costs to "the result to which the program makes the greatest contribution." Where necessary, program costs can be allocated across results. But this should only ever be done on an exception basis. The State of Maryland did this to create a Children's Budget, which turned out to be a useful political tool. And it did not, so far as I know, undermine people's understanding of the relationship between Population and Performance Accountability.

Figure 5.2 provides an entirely different way to go about showing the relationship between programs and population results.

It is a more honest approach and may be just as useful. Programs are shown down the left side, and population results across the top. Each program shows one of four symbols under each result to which it contributes. There are separate symbols for the timing of the contribution (Short Term vs. Long term) and the "power" of the contribution (Direct vs. Indirect). By looking across the columns or down the rows at the "density of ink" one can get a quick sense of the strength of any given set of relationships. Program 1 contributes to 3 population results. Program 2 contributes to just two. The strength and timing of this contribution can be easily read in the symbols. Prosperous economy is supported by all three programs listed. Clean Environment is supported by just one. The chart suggests that job training and child support are strong contributors to Strong Families, but weaker contributors to Safe Communities. (One could imagine

THE CROSS TAB RELATIONSHIP BETWEEN PROGRAMS AND POPULATION RESULTS

	Result 1 Prosperous Economy	Result 2 Clean Environment	Result 3 Safe Communities	Result 4 Strong Families	Result 5 etc.	Result 6 etc.
Program 1 e.g. job training	●		◎	●		
Program 2 e.g. trash recycling	○	●				
Program 3 e.g. child care	◯		○	●		
Program 4 e.g.						
Program 5 e.g.						
Program 6 e.g.						
Program etc. e.g.						

● = ST DIRECT   ◯ = ST INDIRECT   ◎ = LT DIRECT   ○ = LT INDIRECT

Figure 5.2

a chart in this form that summarized the research on such relationships, with hundreds of rows and columns, that could serve as a shopping list for use in creating local Turn the Curve strategies.)

The only time this was ever tried, that I know of, was in a California county where an "X" was put in the box where there was a plausible contribution relationship. Programs quickly realized that the more X's they had the more important they looked. The chart filled up with X's and became useless. But showing something substantive about the relationship (using the four different symbols) gives the chart a much better chance of creating a useful picture. And it may also help teach people about the nature of the relationship between Population and Performance Accountability.

*2. DO YOU ALWAYS HAVE TO TEACH BOTH POPULATION AND PERFORMANCE ACCOUNTABILITY?

Yes. You do. Full stop.[21]

The RBA framework gets used in many different circumstances by many different organizations. What if the organization you are working with is only interested in performance? Do you have to teach Population Accountability or can you skip it? This question comes up a lot in the education community. When working with educators these days, there is an unrelenting focus on school improvement and more specifically turning the curve on achievement test scores. There is often little room for anything else. As you know, it can sometimes be hard to distinguish Population Accountability from Performance Accountability in education, since many school performance measures double as population indicators.

So why not skip teaching population? I have concluded that it is absolutely necessary to teach Population Accountability even if you then turn around, set it aside, and focus exclusively on performance. The reason is this: If you skip Population Accountability (and I have done this a few times and regretted it), the discussion of measures will inevitably come to include a population indicator and it is very difficult to halt the process at this point and explain why population indicators are different from performance measures.

With schools, for example, you will eventually have to talk about the teen pregnancy rate or the rate of teen drug use. These are obviously not performance measures for the schools or any other agency. But what are they? If you haven't set up the indicator category in Population Accountability, the people you are working with are sure to get confused. And that in turn will undermine the discussions of genuine population enterprises such as school community partnerships where people are working on matters bigger than any one agency, like getting children ready for school.

There are comparable reasons for whatever other organization you may be working with. Just to cap off the argument, the distinction between Population and Performance Accountability is the single most important idea in RBA. Why would you teach RBA and skip the most important idea?

---

[21] For those of you lucky enough to have had modern electronics your whole life, this phrase comes from the dark ages of telegraphs and telegrams.

*3. WHEN DO SERVICE SYSTEM PERFORMANCE MEASURES WORK AS POPULATION INDICATORS?

Sometimes it is hard to tell when it is appropriate for a service system performance measure to play the role of population indicator. This happens a lot in health. e.g. rate of Emergency Room usage or Readmission rates to hospital. These are clearly important performance measures for the health care service system. But should they be used as indicators for the population result "Healthy People?" I worked in one situation where one of the partners wanted to use these measures in the 3 to 5 headline measures for Healthy People.

Here's a question that can help you resolve this kind of situation. Consider the result "Healthy People." Ask yourself, if you could make any measure better in the next three years, would the service system performance measure in question rank in the top 10?" Chances are that emergency room usage and readmission rates, however important they may be as performance measures would not compete with rates of cancer, heart disease, diabetes, social determinants of health etc. If a particular service system performance measure doesn't rise to the highest level of importance, it is probably a poor choice as a indicator. This is not a matter of the "status" of a particular measure. The question is how best to use these measures. And they are most helpful in working to improve health services.

*4. DON'T SKIP STEPS BETWEEN POPULATION AND PERFORMANCE ACCOUNTABILITY (Please!)

You need ALL the steps in POPULATION ACCOUNTABILITY thinking process:
Result - Indicator - Baseline - Story - Partners - *What works* - *Strategy* - *Action Plan*

And ALL the steps in PERFORMANCE ACCOUNTABILITY thinking process:
Performance measure - Baseline - Story - Partners - *What works* - *Strategy* - *Action Plan*

PLEASE DON'T MAKE THIS MISTAKE:
Result - Indicator - Strategy - Performance measures

There is a long history of making the mistake: **Result - Indicator - Strategy**. "Here is a problem in society (Result and/or Indicator) and here's how we're going to fix it (Strategy)." No mention of the story behind the indicator baseline. No mention of partners. No mention of what works. Governments and government agencies have been claiming sole responsibility for population results and indicators for decades if not centuries. This is one of the mistakes that RBA, done properly, is designed to correct. Agency after agency, elected official after elected official, go on to promise over-the-top-yet-still-incomplete solutions, with no understanding that the promise itself shuts out partners and makes the work even harder.

The second big mistake in this progression is going directly from **Strategies to Performance measures**. This can mess up the work in two different ways. The first is thinking that performance measures tell you whether a strategy is working. No. No. No. Performance tells you if programs/services are working. If you want to know if your population strategy is working you look at the INDICATORS. Population success is defined by turning the curve on indicators not performance measures. I know of places that have spent hours trying to use the Four Quadrants to develop performance measures for strategies creating enormous confusion and frustration.....because there **are no** performance measures for strategies.

Strategies are made up of many components, some of which will be programs. These programs will need performance measures. And the person managing the strategy will need performance measures to see if implementation is on track. But the success of the strategy itself is determined by whether one or more indicator curves are turned.

*5. RESULTS BASED BUDGETING: "DO WE NEED IT?" "IS IT WORKING?"

These two sentences, 7 words in all, cover everything you need to know about budgeting. Well almost.

When applied to whole programs, the first question (Do we need it?) is a Population Accountability question. Do we need this particular program because it is necessary to the well-being of the people of our nation, state, county, council or city? The deliberations around this question necessarily include the subordinate questions: Can we afford it? Is it needed more than other possible uses of the same money? Can we afford not to do it?

Question 2 (Is it working?) is a Performance Accountability question. This question is asked after we have decided to fund a particular program or policy. Is the program being managed well? (*How well did we do it?*) and more importantly, is it producing the benefits we expect for the people it serves? (*Is anyone better off?*).

Phil Lee has a more clever construction of these two questions. ARE WE DOING THE RIGHT THINGS? ARE WE DOING THINGS RIGHT? If this works better for you, then use it.[22] Either way there is an underlying message here about how the separation of Pop-

---

[22] The only problem is that this wording is "cute," and budget people hate cute..

ulation and Performance Accountability plays out in the budget process. RBA provides a set of methods for answering both questions. The population Turn the Curve thinking process helps us understand what strategies we need to improve quality of life. These strategies can be used to guide the choice of what programs to fund. Performance measures tell us if a program is working or not and the Turn the Curve process guides our thinking about how to improve it.

This is one of the many reasons why formula approaches to budgeting don't work. There is a long history of sometimes well-meaning, and just as often rapacious, consulting companies, coming in and creating elaborate constructs to rank programs by how well they are performing. We have been told that we should "cut programs that aren't working" so we can "fund programs that are working." It sounds logical, except.....whether a program exists in the first place is NOT a matter of its performance (question 2), it's a matter of whether it is "needed" (question 1). If the fire department is not performing well, we don't cut the fire department. We fix it. Because we need it. It plays an important **role** in the quality of life of the community. This is one of the profound implications that comes from understanding the difference between Population and Performance Accountability. And it is a way to guard against the purveyors of formula budgeting.

*6. VALUE FOR MONEY

The term value for money is thrown around a lot these days on both sides of the Atlantic and Pacific as if people actually know what it means. There is the vague suggestion that this concept involves a calculation methodology that can give precise answers about the relative worth of different programs. (Another example of formula budgeting.) And this is where the discussion goes off track. Value for money is not a calculation. It is a judgment about the "value" of a service compared to its cost.

Value for money is a comparison of two things, only one of which can be measured precisely. The comparison is between value which can be approximated in the LR quadrant and unit cost which can be precisely calculated in the UR quadrant. Let's use a mentoring program as our example. The unit cost of a mentoring program can be calculated in a number of different ways, but the most common measure would be the cost per young person. This is calculated by dividing the total cost of the program by the number of young people in the program. Let's say the program costs $50,000 and serves 100 young people. The unit cost is $500 per young person. Is this good or bad? Well you really can't say until you look at the program's LR quadrant outcomes." Here's the best kind of case statement. "This program serves 100 young people. 90% of them show improvements in school attendance and grades and the program only costs $500 per person. Does this sound like a good deal? Yes it does. And that's value for money.

This is sometimes combined into a single measure, cost per outcome or $555 per young person with improved grades and attendance.[23]

Here's why this latter calculation is problematic. It is often used to compare similar programs. We calculate the cost per outcome for 15 different mentoring programs. The one with the highest value for money is the best program and the one with the lowest return is the worst. What is missing here? It is the difference in the characteristics of the young people served by the different programs. Maybe the program with the lowest score is working in a low income neighborhood with the hardest to help young people, while the highest scoring program is working in an upper middle class neighborhood. Maybe the lowest apparent value for money program is the one that is most needed. (See the "degree of difficulty" discussion in Appendix K on "The Performance of Teachers.)

This brings us to the second reason why value for money is not an exact science. The value of anything is a judgment call that can be informed by data but never precisely calculated. Let's take an entirely different example. You are shopping for a car. You are considering three different models each with a different price. The unit cost in this case is obvious since there is only one unit and the total cost of the car is the same as its unit cost. The real question is which car is the best value for the money you are about to spend. Here you will consider gas mileage (another piece of data) but also other harder to quantify features such as comfort, company reputation, resale value, and a dozen others. All these taken together will give you a **sense** of the value which you can then compare to cost.

This is true of the mentoring program too. You will think about the overall value of the program. "Here we have a program working in one of our poorest neighborhoods that is helping young people stay in school and improve their chances of graduation. 65% of the young people graduate compared to only 50% of their peers. And this costs only $500 per young person." Sounds like a good deal to me.

So next time someone tries to pass off the idea that value for money is a calculation, try the mentoring example and, if necessary, the car example......

*7. CUTTING BUDGETS WITH RBA/OBA (Appendix N)

In budgeting, as in life, there are good times and bad times. When we talk about RBA and turning the curve, there is sometimes the presumption that the environment is

---

[23] As a further argument about the deceptive appearance of precision. It is also $555 per young person with improved attendance, better grades, improved relationships with family, reduced liklihood of becoming a teen parent, and possibly many other benefits. It is actually $555 for a package of benefits.

open to new ideas, new programs, new uses of money. This is, of course, not always the case. Sometimes the challenge in front of us is not how to grow the budget but how to cut it. Even in the best years, some things must be pruned. If adding to the budget can be thought of in terms of doing the most good, then cutting the budget can be thought of as doing the least harm.

Appendix N provides two exercises that show how RBA can be used to cut budgets so as to do the least harm. One exercise addresses the question at the population level. "How can we cut the budget so that it does the least harm to the quality of life of the people of this (city, county, state or nation)?" The second exercise looks inside a given program and asks "How can we cut this particular program so that it does the least harm to the program's customers?"

I hope you never have to use these exercises. But if you have to cut the budget, you may find that these are more disciplined and constructive conversations than the haphazard way it is usually done. Remember that budgeting is a political process and rational analysis of this sort may have no bearing the final decisions. Results based budgeting does not guarantee that you will **make** better choices. All it can do is **provide** better choices.

*8. QUESTIONS ABOUT SOCIAL INVESTING (Appendix O)

When I worked as CFO of Maryland's welfare and social services agency a million years ago, I was part of several successful social investment efforts which paid for themselves from savings elsewhere in our budget. The most important of these was the Department's investment in one of the country's first Family Preservation programs. This was an intensive program modeled on the Homebuilders Program in Seattle that worked with families to keep children safely at home and avoid expensive placement in foster care. We were able to show that the savings in foster care more than paid for the program. That analysis won us the support and approval of the State budget office and the Legislative budget committees. I helped to manage a similar investment effort that helped recipients of state General Assistance apply for and obtain federal disability assistance. The savings in the 100% state funded General Assistance program was more than enough to pay the costs of helping these people get the benefits to which they were entitled. In another effort we worked with the state Health Department to move people from state mental hospitals to a community based program called Project Home. This was paid for by closing hospital wards one at a time and transferring the associated funding from the Health department's budget to ours.

On the basis of these experiences, I wrote a proposal to create a "Governor's Investment Board" which would front the money for these kinds of promising social investments. The money would be repaid from savings (calculated to include cost savings and cost avoidance) and the "profit" share would be returned to the fund. Governments do this kind of investing all the time. We invest in preventive maintenance. We invest in energy efficient buildings. We invest in new business development. But good social sector ideas are often left on the sidelines because the returns are less certain or can not be produced within a one or two year budget window. A government investment board could provide the gap financing for good ideas that are riskier or take a longer time to pay off. And it could bring to bear sophisticated modeling and other techniques to show where and how to capture the savings. The Governor at the time was not interested in this idea (that is another story) but the proposal, which is still a good one, can be found on the FPSI publications page.

There is a lot of talk these days, in the US, UK and Australia, about social investments that claim to produce not just public benefits but also savings sufficient to pay private investors a profit. Accompanying this talk is also a lot of wishful thinking. The paper in Appendix O is based on my own experience with social investing and outlines some of the tough questions that must be answered for these kinds of deals to work.

*9. BEWARE OF SOCIAL RETURN ON INVESTMENT (SROI)

Any cost/benefit or return-on-investment analysis consists of two parts. Part 1 is an inventory of where the benefits of the subject program or service show up in society. This step can be useful in its own right in explaining why a program is potentially valuable and worth funding.

The second step is the hard part. This requires attaching a dollar value to each benefit. In business ROI, these benefits take the form of tangible income and assets which offsets expenses and produce profit. In social ventures, the matter of attaching a dollar value to a program benefit is much more complicated. (I address some of the techniques for producing cost/benefit analyses in TH pp. 133-35 / 139 - 141)

There are now companies promoting an approach called Social Return on Investment (SROI) that use highly suspect methods for attaching dollar value to social benefits. I have had the opportunity to review SROI calculations for three programs. In one example, a consulting firm assessed the value of a food bank operation. They concluded that having more food on the table helped families do a better job of raising their children (OK so far.). But then they credited a large portion of the average cost of raising a child (more than $200,000 over 18 years) as a social benefit somehow produced by the food bank program. This is absurd on its face. Yet this assumption was buried in a mass of calculations that were hard for the funders who purchased this service to see and understand. The resulting number looked impressive. The food bank returned more than $17 in SROI for every dollar spent. The funder in essence paid for this single number to be produced. But when you look behind the curtain (as in Oz) you find the methodology was a joke. It took me a long time searching SROI sites on the web to find even this one example of the precise estimation methodology employed.

I was later asked by a large nonprofit organization to provide a confidential review of two other SROI calculations. In one of these cases, a set of assumptions, similar to the food bank, were combined to produce a $23 social return for the program. In a stunning conclusion, the analyst stated that $23.00 "sounded too high." (I am not making this up.) And so the SROI was arbitrarily reduced to $2.30. Any methodology that can be off by an entire order of magnitude must be considered suspect. The organization paid the consultant a lot of money for the production of this entirely made up number. The exact details of SROI calculations are often hidden from view. Before you decide to pay for this work, make sure you have an impartial financial professional examine several examples of the exact methodology used by the consultant in previous work. In the three cases I studied, the final SROI number was based on highly questionable assumptions and methodologies. Anyone with a budget and finance background will be able to see through these problems immediately.

10. A Q&A SESSION with WALES: July 2010
with thanks to Matt Jenkins and Adrian Davies (Appendix P)

In a growing number of places, RBA is used widely enough that it makes sense to organize a community of practice where people can come together to share experiences and ask questions. I really enjoy interacting with these groups. The participants come up with the most interesting questions. Here is a great Q&A exchange with partners from across Wales.

11. Eighteen Short Bits of Advice
Including some important points from the essays above

1. Remember the option to collect data on a sample basis.
2. Make sure data collection instruments are USEFUL to the line worker, and not an imposition on the client or worker.
3. Meet your own needs for data and reporting. Then consider the funder's requirements.
4. If a funder asks you to do something that doesn't make sense, don't do it. Talk to the funder and explain why. Chances are they will agree.
5. Remember the importance of stories in reporting progress. Build a collection of success stories.
6. Put data on the wall so that staff and customers can see it. One of them might ask "What's the difference between a positive and negative exit?"

7. "What difference did we make?" is a causality claim. Chances are you made a contribution. You can't "prove" causality without expensive research, and even then it is often inconclusive.

8. Read "Trying Hard Is Not Good Enough" more than once. Even RBA experts forget stuff. Read it in bite size pieces as part of a book club type group.

9. Do not use data to pass judgment on programs but rather to make them better.

10. Do not buy into any method that appears to make budgeting and cost benefit analysis easy or formulaic.

11. Remember two questions: "If your work is wildly successful, what number gets better? If you could make one number better in the next 3 years, what would it be?"

12. Services are not a substitute for income. Good stable jobs will reduce most social problems. Someday I want to write the book "Let Them Eat Services."

13. Start building affordable housing and stop just talking about it.

14. Never pretend to have all the answers. Admit when you don't know something. We're all learning.

15. Stop Planning to plan to plan - get on with the Turn the Curve process.

16. Don't use the measure % of goals met. It means nothing to the outside world. Instead identify the most common goals, e.g. employment, and report % of people who got a job, for whom employment was a goal.

17. Basic cell/mobile phone service these days is cheap and the ability to be connected in this way will eventually be considered a human right. Consider making it part of the package of services that you deliver to vulnerable and socially isolated customers

18. We will eventually empty our prisons the same way we emptied mental hospitals decades ago. The tragedy with mental hospitals was that we failed to provide the full range of necessary services and supports in the community. Let's get on with reducing the non-violent population in our prisons and not make the same mistake of failing to provide the needed community services.

CHAPTER 6:

The Results Scorecard (Appendix Q)

by Marc Stone and Kayleigh Weaver

The Results Scorecard is one of the most important tools for practitioners since the beginning of RBA more than 20 years ago. It is perfectly aligned with RBA concepts, which means it can help individual programs separately track Population and Performance Accountability (the single most important idea in RBA). It also helps funders and large organizations manage data across complex service networks, with simple comprehensible reporting processes. It produces ready-to-use Turn the Curve reports. And much more. Any description of the Scorecard will sound like an advertisement. Sorry about that. Check it out for yourself.

1. Overview:

The Results Scorecard is a strategic decision-making support software developed by the Results Leadership Group, LLC in 2010. It has been designed specifically to help non-profits and government agencies implement the RBA framework and create collective, measurable impact for organizations and communities. It does so by connecting all stakeholders in a single interactive network, providing rapid access to critical data, and creating visual dashboards of knowledge that can be used to improve decision-making, drive strategies, and accelerate the RBA process. The software uses a simple and intuitive design, and the language is customizable to support each user's unique terminology.

Currently, the Results Scorecard has over 1,500 active users representing more than 260 organizations from over 15 countries. Users include clients like the Promise Neighborhoods Institute, The Campaign for Grade Level Reading, The U.S Department of Education, the City of Baltimore, various United Ways, The New Zealand Government, and many more.

2. Real-Time, Interactive Scorecards:

With the Results Scorecard's interactive scorecards, you can monitor Population Results and Indicators, as well as the Programs and Performance Measures that are part of your strategy to improve. You have the ability to "zoom-out" and see the big picture, or "zoom-in" to see data values and trend lines for individual Indicators and Performance Measures. Selecting any measure from the Scorecard will allow you to access the Turn the Curve view for that measure. In the Turn the Curve view, you can input the components of the RBA talk-to-action process including the Story Behind the Curve, Partners, What Works, and Action-Plans.

On the graphs themselves, you can add data values and color bands, analyze your curve, and show targets where applicable. It is also possible to create a forecast by simply drawing it onto the graph with your mouse. When you are happy with your graphs, you can export them in a variety of formats (.jpeg, .png, .pdf, etc.) to be included in reports and presentations.

In the Scorecard, you can easily compare data from different client populations, using the compare-and-contrast function. This allows you to combine multiple measures on a single graph, so that you can make comparisons and develop insights about the relationships between your data-sets. This is useful for all kinds of programs, but it is especially useful for organizations that place a focus on advancing equity.

Finally, the ability to embed your Scorecards on websites makes it easy to share your data with partners, funders. Your embedded Scorecards are live, meaning that when you make a change or add more data, those changes are automatically reflected on your website.

3. Strategy-Maps and Gantt Charts

The Results Scorecard Strategy Mapping feature allows organizations to create a visual representation of the connections between individual efforts and the Collective Impact they hope to achieve on Results and Indicators. Strategy Maps are invaluable tools for bringing people together to quickly build consensus on what work needs to be done and how everyone contributes.

In the Results Scorecard, Strategy Maps are automatically populated with the Results and Programs from your Scorecard, making it easier for you to get started. You can then visually arrange your Results and Programs onto a freeform canvas that can be enhanced with arrows, images, colors, texts, hyperlinks, attachments, and more. The entire Strategy Map is interactive, so clicking on your Results and Programs lets you instantly drill into the operational level and see your measures. Just like Scorecards, Strategy Maps can be embedded on websites or exported to be included in reports and presentations.

With Results Scorecard's Automated Gantt Charts, you can easily manage your projects and assign actions to individual users. This will help you stay organized, accountable, and timely when executing your RBA action-plan. The Gantt chart function is another powerful tool for turning complex projects into an organized breakdown of component parts, which are displayed on a timeline. They are especially useful for communications and planning, since drawing out complex plans into consecutive steps makes those plans easier to understand.

Gantt Charts can also show project progress by displaying the completion status of actions. The Gantt chart automatically arranges your Actions under the Result, Indicator, and/or Performance Measure to which they contribute. For any given Indicator or Performance Measure, you can view all the actions associated with that measure in the timeline.

Individuals interested in trying the Results Scorecard can sign up for a free, 30-day trial of the software at www.resultsscorecard.com.

4. Selected Examples of Scorecard reports (Appendix Q)

This provides a quick view of two of the most important types of reports that are possible using the Scorecard. The first shows population and performance data for a single program of the Lamoille Family Services in Morrisville, Vermont. (Thanks to Scott Johnson for permission to show this report). The second example shows a Turn the Curve view for a particular measure, in this case a population indicator concerning rates of smoking. These reports show how complex data from many different programs can be corralled into a common structure and then used to drive program performance and quality of life improvement.

The press release in Appendix R comes from the New Zealand Ministry for Business, Innovation and Employment and illustrates some of the benefits of the Scorecard. It also shows the extent of RBA usage across New Zealand, one of the countries where RBA usage is most advanced.

APPENDICES

Note that there is some duplication in the appendices between this volume and the 10th Anniversary Edition of TH, and there is a good reason for this. I do not expect that everyone who has purchased TH will buy the 10th Anniversary Edition. And yet I want you to have access to some of the most important changes in that book. Hence the Tool for Choosing a Common Language, the RBA Self Assessment Questionnaire, and the Readings and Resources Appendices are duplicated in this volume. In theory of course, everything is online. But there is now so much about RBA online it is hard to know what is more or less important. The things in these appendices are some of those that should not get lost in the crowd.

A. Vermont Accountability Compact

B. Vermont Act 186: An act relating to reporting on population-level outcomes and indicators and on program-level performance measures.

C. *How outcomes saved my life (or at least my sanity)* by Mike Pinnock

D. *Transforming Life Chances for Children, Young People and Families in Leeds, UK Using Outcomes-Based Accountability*, by Nigel Richardson and Adam Hewitt

E. Tool for Choosing a Common Language

F. Mental Models

G. RBA Implementation Self Assessment Questionnaire

H. Collective Impact using RBA

I. Next Generation Contracting

J. *The Cardiff and Vale Experience* by Ruth Jordan

K. Additional Notes on Teacher Performance Evaluation

L. How to measure Alignment

M. RBA on RBA in Anglicare Western Australia by Desiree Nangle plus supplemental research questions

N. Cutting Budgets with RBA

O. Social Investment Bonds and the Challenges of Social Investing

P. A Q&A Session with Wales

Q. Examples of Scorecards

R Press release: *NZ Government Chooses Results Scorecard™ Software to Manage Streamlined Contracting with NGO's*

S. Selected Readings and Resources

Notices regarding the use of Results-Based Accountability™ (RBA) material

THE VERMONT ACCOUNTABILITY COMPACT

This Compact honors the long Vermont tradition of partners working together to improve the quality of life of our people and our communities. The Compact signals our intent to promote a culture of accountability in pursuit of those ends.

Due to the long history of Results-Based Accountability™ in Vermont, its widespread and growing application across the nonprofit and state sectors, and our belief in the collective impact of a shared framework, the Compact features an RBA approach. We recognize that there are many alternative pathways to greater accountability and welcome all efforts to that end.

By signing the Compact, we commit to support, promote, and regularly assess our progress on the implementation of a culture of accountability in our work.

HOW WE THINK AND TALK

1. Language Discipline

    a. Using core language discipline across the public, private and nonprofit sectors in order to work together effectively.

    b. Understanding the difference between two levels of accountability: population and program performance.

    c. Using specific language around measurement, including:

        i. Population results or population outcomes to reference population-level quality of life conditions,

        ii. Indicators to reference the class of measures that tell if those population-level conditions are getting better or worse, and

        iii. Performance measures to separately reference the class of measures that tell if programs, agencies and services systems are working.

d. For our performance measures, using a framework focused on customer outcomes that asks: How much did we do? How well did we do it? Is anyone better off?

e. Understanding and using baseline data with history and forecasting so that we define success as turning the curve rather than comparing to a single point in time.

2. Training to Support a Shift in Culture

a. Providing RBA training to build common understanding of concepts, foster core language discipline, and create a culture of working together to make a difference.

b. Building in-house capacity to train and support the use of RBA as part of a larger program of organizational and professional development.

3. Communications

a. Promoting efforts to "spread the word" about RBA concepts and practices.

b. Building and participating in an RBA learning collaborative or community of practice.

c. Developing shared messaging amongst public, private and nonprofit entities to communicate our practices relative to Population and Performance Accountability.

WHAT WE DO

1. Infrastructure Improvements

a. Working with funders and grantees to simplify and standardize grant applications and grant reporting.

b. Reviewing our forms to ensure consistency with an outcomes-based approach.

2. Planning and Budgeting

a. Designing strategic plans to reflect our role in improving community or population-level quality of life, and using performance measures to show how well we are fulfilling that role.

b. Ensuring that budgeting systems support our role in improving population-level quality of life, and support our use of performance measures, with a focus on customer outcomes, to improve the quality of our services.

c. Using data transparently to track and drive performance.

d. Creating a Data Development Agenda and an Information and Research Agenda to support our growth as a learning organization.

3. Making our Progress Visible

a. Developing visible strategies to reinforce Performance Accountability, including charts on the walls, and 3 to 5 measures for each level of programming.

b. Using data on a regular basis for supervision, program oversight and grant and contract reporting.

4. Partnering

a. Building a network amongst public, private and nonprofit partners to improve the community's quality of life.

b. Using population outcomes to articulate community ambitions and population indicators to assess progress and plan for the future.

c. Partnering with communities, especially our customers, to improve our services and help others improve theirs.

APPENDIX B (See Chapter 1, Essay 4)

VERMONT ACT 186

No. 186. An act relating to reporting on population-level outcomes and indicators and on program-level performance measures. (S.293)

It is hereby enacted by the General Assembly of the State of Vermont:

Sec. 1. PURPOSE
  (a) This act is necessary for the General Assembly to obtain data-based information to know how well State government is working to achieve the population-level outcomes the General Assembly sets for Vermont's quality of life, and will assist the General Assembly in determining how best to invest taxpayer dollars.
  (b) Evaluating the results of spending taxpayer dollars will allow the General Assembly to be more forward-thinking, strategic, and responsive to the long-term needs of Vermonters and allow the Executive Branch to consider how the programs it administers could be further refined in order to produce better results.
  (c) Using the data-based information provided under this act will encourage State government to continue to move steadily toward results-based accountability and will help educate the General Assembly and Executive Branch on how to be more effective and accountable to Vermonters and will encourage a better partnership with Vermont communities.

§ 2311. CHIEF PERFORMANCE OFFICER; ANNUAL REPORT ON POPULATION-LEVEL OUTCOMES USING INDICATORS

(a) Report. Annually, on or before July 30, the Chief Performance Officer within the Agency of Administration shall report to the General Assembly on the State's progress in reaching the population-level outcomes for each area of Vermont's quality of life set forth in subsection (b) of this section by providing data for the population-level indicators that are requested pursuant to the process set forth in subsection (c) of this section.

(b) Vermont population-level quality of life outcomes.
    (1) Vermont has a prosperous economy.
    (2) Vermonters are healthy.
    (3) Vermont's environment is clean and sustainable.
    (4) Vermont's communities are safe and supportive.
    (5) Vermont's families are safe, nurturing, stable, and supported.

      (6) Vermont's children and young people achieve their potential, including:
         (A) Pregnant women and young people thrive.
         (B) Children are ready for school.
         (C) Children succeed in school.
         (D) Youths choose healthy behaviors.
         (E) Youths successfully transition to adulthood.
      (7) Vermont's elders and people with disabilities and people with mental conditions live with dignity and independence in settings they prefer.
      (8) Vermont has open, effective, and inclusive government at the State and local levels.
   (c) Requesting population-level indicators.
      (1) Annually, on or before March 1, a standing committee of the General Assembly having jurisdiction over a population-level quality of life outcome set forth in subsection (b) of this section may submit to the Government Accountability Committee a request that any population-level indicator related to that outcome be revised.
      (2) If that request is approved by the Government Accountability Committee, the President Pro Tempore of the Senate, and the Speaker of the House, the Chief Performance Officer shall revise and report on the population-level indicator in accordance with the request and this section.
   (d) The report set forth in this section shall not be subject to the limitation on the duration of agency reports set forth in 2 V.S.A. § 20(d).

§ 2312. PERFORMANCE ACCOUNTABILITY LIAISONS TO THE GENERAL ASSEMBLY

   (a) The Chief Performance Officer shall designate an employee in each agency of State government to be a Performance Accountability liaison to the General Assembly. A liaison designated under this section shall be responsible for reviewing with the General Assembly any of the population-level outcomes and indicators set forth in section 2311 of this subchapter to which that agency contributes and for responding to any other requests for results-based accountability information requested by the General Assembly.
   (b) The Performance Accountability liaisons shall report to the Chief Performance Officer on any action taken under subsection (a) of this section.
   (c) Annually, on or before July 30 and as part of any other report requirement to the General Assembly set forth in this subchapter, the Chief Performance Officer shall report to the General Assembly on his or her analysis of the actions taken by the Performance Accountability liaisons under this section.

§ 2313. PERFORMANCE CONTRACTS AND GRANTS

   (a) The Chief Performance Officer shall assist agencies as necessary in developing performance measures for contracts and grants.

(b) Annually, on or before July 30 and as part of any other report requirement to the General Assembly set forth in this subchapter, the Chief Performance Officer shall report to the General Assembly on the progress by rate or percent of how many State contracts and grants have Performance Accountability requirements and the rate or percent of contractors' and grantees' compliance with those requirements.

Sec. 3. INITIAL POPULATION-LEVEL INDICATORS

Until any population-level indicators are requested pursuant to the provisions of Sec. 2 of this act, 3 V.S.A. § 2311(c) (requesting population-level indicators), each population-level quality of life outcome set forth in Sec. 2 of this act, 3 V.S.A. § 2311(b) (Vermont population-level quality of life outcomes), and listed in this section shall have the following population-level indicators:

(1) Vermont has a prosperous economy.
  (A) percent or rate per 1,000 jobs of nonpublic sector employment;
  (B) median household income;
  (C) percent of Vermont covered by state-of-the-art telecommunications infrastructure;
  (D) median house price;
  (E) rate of resident unemployment per 1,000 residents;
  (F) percent of structurally-deficient bridges, as defined by the Vermont Agency of Transportation; and
  (G) percent of food sales that come from Vermont farms.

(2) Vermonters are healthy.
  (A) percent of adults 20 years of age or older who are obese;
  (B) percent of adults smoking cigarettes;
  (C) number of adults who are homeless;
  (D) percent of individuals and families living at different poverty levels;
  (E) percent of adults at or below 200 percent of federal poverty level; and
  (F) percent of adults with health insurance.

(3) Vermont's environment is clean and sustainable.
  (A) cumulative number of waters subject to TMDLs or alternative pollution control plans;
  (B) percent of water, sewer, and stormwater systems that meet federal and State standards;
  (C) carbon dioxide per capita; and
  (D) electricity by fuel or power type.

(4) Vermont's communities are safe and supportive.
  (A) rate of petitions granted for relief from domestic abuse per 1,000 residents;
  (B) rate of violent crime per 1,000 crimes;
  (C) rate of sexual assault committed against residents per 1,000 residents;

(D) percent of residents living in affordable housing;

(E) percent or rate per 1,000 people convicted of crimes of recidivism;

(F) incarceration rate per 100,000 residents; and

(G) percent or rate per 1,000 residents of residents entering the corrections system.

(5) Vermont's families are safe, nurturing, stable, and supported.

(A) number and rate per 1,000 children of substantiated reports of child abuse and neglect;

(B) number of children who are homeless;

(C) number of families that are homeless; and

(D) number and rate per 1,000 children and youth of children and youth in out-of-home care.

(6) Vermont's children and young people achieve their potential, including:

(A) Pregnant women and young people thrive.

(i) percent of women who receive first trimester prenatal care;

(ii) percent of live births that are preterm (less than 37 weeks);

(iii) rate of infant mortality per 1,000 live births;

(iv) percent of children at or below 200 percent of federal poverty level; and

(v) percent of children with health insurance.

(B) Children are ready for school.

(i) percent of kindergarteners fully immunized with all five vaccines required for school.

(ii) percent of first-graders screened for vision and hearing problems;

(iii) percent of children ready for school in all five domains of healthy development; and

(iv) percent of children receiving State subsidy enrolled in high quality early childhood programs that receive at least four out of five stars under State standards.

(C) Children succeed in school.

(i) rate of school attendance per 1,000 children;

(ii) percent of children below the basic level of fourth grade reading achievement under State standards; and

(iii) rate of high school graduation per 1,000 high school students.

(D) Youths choose healthy behaviors.

(i) rate of pregnancy per 1,000 females 15-17 years of age;

(ii) rate of pregnancy per 1,000 females 18-19 years of age;

(iii) percent of adolescents smoking cigarettes;

(iv) percent of adolescents who used marijuana in the past 30 days;

(v) percent of adolescents who reported ever using a prescription drug without a prescription;

(vi) percent of adolescents who drank alcohol in the past 30 days;

(vii) number and rate per 1,000 minors of minors who are under the supervision of the Department of Corrections.

(E) Youths successfully transition to adulthood.
    (i) percent of high school seniors with plans for education, vocational training, or employment;
    (ii) percent of graduating high school seniors who continue their education within six months of graduation;
    (iii) percent of all deaths for youths 10-19 years of age;
    (iv) rate of suicide per 100,000 Vermonters;
    (v) percent of adolescents with a suicide attempt that requires medical attention;
    (vi) percent of high school graduates entering postsecondary education, work, or training;
    (vii) percent of completion of postsecondary education; and
    (viii) rate of high school graduates entering a training program per 1,000 high school graduates.

(7) Vermont's elders and people with disabilities and people with mental conditions live with dignity and independence in settings they prefer.
    (A) rate of confirmed reports of abuse and neglect of vulnerable adults per 1,000 vulnerable adults;
    (B) percent of elders living in institutions versus receiving home care; and
    (C) number of people with disabilities and people with mental conditions receiving State services living in each of the following: institutions, residential or group facilities, or independently.

(8) Vermont has open, effective, and inclusive government at the State and local levels.
    (A) percent of youth who spoke to their parents about school;
    (B) percent of youth who report they help decide what goes on in their school;
    (C) percent of eligible population voting in general elections;
    (D) percent of students volunteering in their community in the past week;
    (E) percent of youth who feel valued by their community; and
    (F) percent of youth that report their teachers care about them and give them encouragement.

Sec. 4. CHIEF PERFORMANCE OFFICER; REPORT ON PERFORMANCE MEASURE PILOT PROGRAM

(a) Annually, on or before July 30 and as part of any other report requirement to the General Assembly set forth in Sec. 2 of this act, 3 V.S.A. chapter 45, subchapter 5 (Chief Performance Officer), the Chief Performance Officer shall submit to the General Assembly a report on the Department of Finance and Management's Performance Measure Pilot Program. The report shall include:
(1) the performance measure data collected by the pilot participants; and

(2) the progress of all programs in the Executive Branch and how many of those programs have and are using performance measures.
(b) The Chief Performance Officer shall collaborate with the Joint Fiscal Office in developing new performance measures for programs.

Sec. 6. CHIEF PERFORMANCE OFFICER; INITIAL PERFORMANCE ACCOUNTABILITY LIAISON APPOINTMENTS

The Chief Performance Officer within the Agency of Administration shall make his or her initial designations of the Performance Accountability liaisons described in Sec. 2 of this act, 3 V.S.A. § 2312, by November 15, 2014.

Sec. 7. QUARTERLY PROGRESS REPORTS; TEMPORARY SUSPENSION

The report requirement set forth in 2010 Acts and Resolves No. 146, Sec. H4 (Challenges for Change; quarterly reporting and implementation) is temporarily suspended. The report requirement shall resume in 2017 beginning with the first quarterly report due for that year.

§ 2312. PERFORMANCE ACCOUNTABILITY LIAISONS TO THE GENERAL ASSEMBLY

(a) The Chief Performance Officer shall designate an employee in each agency of State government to be a Performance Accountability liaison to the General Assembly. A liaison designated under this section shall be responsible for reviewing with the General Assembly any of the population-level outcomes and indicators set forth in section 2311 of this subchapter to which that agency contributes and for responding to any other requests for results-based accountability information requested by the General Assembly.
(b) The Performance Accountability liaisons shall report to the Chief Performance Officer on any action taken under subsection (a) of this section.
(c) Annually, on or before July 30 and as part of any other report requirement to the General Assembly set forth in this subchapter, the Chief Performance Officer shall report to the General Assembly on his or her analysis of the actions taken by the Performance Accountability liaisons under this section.

Sec. 10. EFFECTIVE DATES

(a) This section and Secs. 1 (purpose)-7 (quarterly progress reports; temporary suspension) shall take effect on passage. No. 186 Page 13 of 13
(b) Secs. 8 (repeal; annual report on population-level outcomes using indicators) and 9 (amending 3 V.S.A. § 2312 (Performance Accountability liaisons to the General Assembly)) shall take effect on January 1, 2017.

Date Governor signed bill: June 11, 2014

APPENDIX C (See Chapter 1, Essay 9)

How outcomes saved my life (or at least my sanity)

Mike Pinnock

I've just been directed towards what Lee, my Senior Tyre Technician, is referring to as 'the Customer Comfort Zone'. I'm waiting for a tyre to arrive that I was told was already in stock. I have trouble in locating the zone at first because it looks pretty much like the other three corners of this dingy garage. However, I soon realise that the presence of a few plastic seats and some dog-eared copies of *Hello*! magazine, (together with the [almost] total absence of dangerous hydraulic machinery) denote it's special status.

Earlier today I'd been sitting in the waiting room of an Ear, Nose and Throat clinic. My ear hurt. The appointment system was a shambles. My fellow sufferers were using whatever faculties they had left between them to berate Paula, the beleaguered receptionist, who in turn, was blaming 'the system'. I was doing my bit for the common cause that had come to unite us. Eventually I was advised that today's session was over-running so I should go home and await a further appointment. Resigned to my fate, I was at the point of climbing peaceably down from the reception desk into the welcoming arms of the security staff when I noticed that I'd been recorded as 'DNA' on my appointment card. When pressed to explain why I was being recorded on the system as, 'Did Not Attend', when I was clearly very much in attendance, Paula eventually confided in me that she didn't like doing it, but management insisted that they "recorded overflow as DNA". So now it was official. I am overflow. Overflow that was escorted off the premises. Ears still ringing.

Perhaps my 'customer journey' through these services sounds familiar to you. Or perhaps not.

> *The metrics spoke of a place where customers were given a choice of appointment times; a place where customers didn't have to wait; a place where people were treated courteously in pleasing surroundings.*

Maybe I just caught them on a bad day. The 'performance information' proudly displayed on the notice boards certainly suggests that this was probably the case. The neat little charts boasted of "upper quartile performance throughout the customer journey based on a range of customer-valued metrics". The metrics spoke of a place where customers were given a choice of appointment times; a place where customers didn't have to wait; a place where people were treated courteously in pleasing surroundings. And of course, a place where pigs swooped and soared in the aquamarine skies above.

Watching the young staff in these settings, I reflected on my early days as a trainee social worker. I was 18 years old, spotty and earnest when I started. And I still had that annoying childhood habit of asking 'why?' Up until that point, my experience of work had had a pleasing symmetry to it: Leave home and go to the newsagent; fill bag with newspapers; empty bag by matching scribble on newspaper to addresses; go home. Starting work in a busy social work office, I found myself thrown into a world of boundless uncertainty and uncertain boundaries.

I'd already decided at school that I wanted to be a social worker. Like countless others before me, I had a vague idea that I'd be able to 'make a difference' in some small way. These were the days of 'generic' caseloads, so I soon found myself working with families, older people, people with disability, mental health problems. What I slowly realised was that I had no idea what the difference I wanted to make might look like or how I might make it – let alone how I'd know if I was making

107

it. I found myself working in a world without outcomes.

My sense of hopelessness grew with the size of my caseload and the gravity of the cases assigned to me. By the age of 23, I had a caseload of 120. Over the preceding years I'd been held at knifepoint, called to the local mortuary to identify a dead baby, and delivered more modified toilet seats than was good for a young man.

> *What I slowly realised was that I had no idea what the difference I wanted to make might look like or how I might make it – let alone how I'd know if it was making it. I found myself working in a world without outcomes.*

My salvation eventually came when I began to specialise in working with young offenders. Whilst working in this service we developed a very simple way of understanding our purpose: stop young people getting into crime, court, custody and care. Although these weren't outcomes in the way that we understand them today, the experience taught me a lot about the value of giving meaning to work through unambiguous and durable statements of purpose. We had intuitively developed what Peter Senge described in his book *The Fifth Discipline* (1990) as "a Shared Vision".

We went on to develop a whole range of targeted programmes to help realise this vision and, by the early 1980s, we'd introduced an early example of systems monitoring in children's services. Every event was lovingly recorded each week on a computer that looked like something off the set of *Star Trek*. For the first time in my fledgling career I was happy. And so were the people I worked with. We had a clear understanding of 'the difference' we wanted to make. We had developed a set of practices that we believed in. We had a clear idea about the partners we would need to work with to achieve our goals, and we had a system in place that allowed us to judge whether or not we were achieving them. From this point onwards, the idea of outcomes in children's services became my muse.

Fast-forward 30 years, and it feels like outcome-orientated practices in children's social care services have always been with us. Indeed, I now find myself working with a generation of practitioners and managers in England who have known nothing else – the *Every Child Matters* outcomes have been a reference point throughout their careers.

This is where the happy ending should come. Sadly that is not to be.

Over the past 15 years I've seen the simple idea of evaluating outcomes in social care recklessly damaged by its association with the arrogant excesses of so-called 'performance management'. For many, the very idea of measuring progress has become a tyranny. Each week the media brings us yet another example of some cynical management contrivance for creating the impression of 'improved performance'. But just like the little trick of recording my aborted visit to the clinic as 'Did Not Attend', it often creates an unreliable impression of the service it purports to represent.

Like many people, I have come to regard this so-called 'performance management' culture as just that. A shabby little bit of theatre that often bears no relation to the real experiences of the service users and carers it exists to serve. Certainly it was clear that neither Lee nor Paula were comfortable with their roles in this performance, or the lines they'd been given to recite (but all credit to Paula for going 'off script'). If anything, being expected to maintain the pretence of a service that is something it's not, probably compounds the drudgery that has become their daily experience of work.

As a long-standing advocate of outcome-based practices, I've found myself questioning whether I've been an unwitting accomplice to this charade. Have the ideas that I've advocated for with such enthusiasm over the past 25 years really brought us to this? My recent participation in a national review of child protection arrangements in the UK gave me the opportunity for a personal stock-take. The review, led by Professor Eileen Munro, has created a mood in the UK for 'reclaiming social work' from the overbearing bureaucracy that has come to blight it. Taking my cue from this, I've started to think about the prospect of 'reclaiming outcomes' from the army of auditors, accountants and inspectors that have appropriated them.

So why do we measure? In theory, the feedback that measurement gives us should serve two primary purposes: the external purpose of accountability, and the internal purpose of organisational learning. However, the masterful dissembling that we have seen going into the external reporting of performance tells us that these are often conflicting, rather than complementary, purposes.

> *In theory, the feedback that measurement gives us should serve two primary purposes: the external purpose of accountability, and the internal purpose of organisational learning.*

So, you might well ask, why bother? Why does it matter? Has the damage not been done? Well the answer is that I still believe that there is something special in the idea of outcome-orientated approaches to working with children and young people – something that can help build resilience in individuals, within teams and across teams and provide a touchstone for helping make decisions – big and small.

In the section that follows, I've tried to imagine how I could convince Lee and Paula – or anyone about to embark on a career in social work – why outcomes are important and how I think they can help them in their careers.

What's special about outcomes?

The seven C's of outcomes

- Clear – they're easily understood by both professional and lay audiences
- Child-centred – they're about children's lives – not management's 'mission'
- Concise – they give us a memorable and portable vision of a desired future
- Consensual – they describe a shared purpose that everyone can sign up to
- Constant – they remain constant over time and place

- Comprehensive – they encourage us to see the 'whole child'
- Challenging – they're inspirational as well as aspirational

Clarity of purpose

Outcomes bring meaning to our work. Without this meaning, there is only activity. They begin to answer those awkward "why?" questions. By being able to describe the purpose of our collective work with children and young people in a simple statement of desired outcomes, we can bring a shared meaning to our efforts – across a team, a service area, an organisation or a whole community partnership.

Outcomes help guide our collective thinking and frame our collective actions. They help us to find a way out of the labyrinth of processes that we can so easily become lost in. Like Ariadne's golden thread, we should be able to follow the path of all of our processes to the outcomes that they exist to support. If we can't find a clear path back to an outcome, then we need to question the value of the process in question.

> *Managing children's services is not the same as managing a pizza delivery service. Better outcomes are not commodities that are delivered to the doors of eagerly awaiting families. Outcomes in children's services are always "work in progress" – progress that is usually made against great adversity. To see better outcomes as anything less would be doing a great injustice to the children and young people whose life-chances we're hoping to improve. (Pinnock, 2011)*

The work of Mark Friedman has had a massive impact on the movement towards outcome-orientated partnership work here in the UK. Friedman's Results Based Accountability (RBA©, or Outcome Based Accountability [OBA], as it is referred to in England) approach is also influencing government and non-governmental work in many other countries around the world. His starting place for engaging people on outcome-based work is to develop a common language with a common meaning. This makes the approach accessible and wholly inclusive. I've seen senior government Ministers sitting alongside street-wise activists using OBA to tackle a wide range of community issues.

Used in the right way, outcomes give people a set of simple ideas to organise their individual and collective efforts around. The work that I referred to earlier with young people in trouble led to a dramatic reduction in the numbers of young people entering the formal juvenile justice system. The outcomes we set for ourselves gave us a clear starting place for measuring progress. The progress we were able to demonstrate was just as important in winning over sceptics as it was sustaining the motivation of the converts. Note that we didn't have to wait months or years for some annual return to be published. We got real figures in real time – and because measuring the things that matter was something we did for ourselves – rather than something that was 'done to us', the idea of manipulating the data never even entered our heads. This experience underlies the importance of being clear about not just what you are measuring – but why you are measuring it.

When we take an outcome focus in our partnership work, it helps us to re-connect to our vocation and to keep those children, young people and their families at the forefront of our thinking and our actions.

> *We want measurement to be used from a deeper place of understanding, the understanding that the real capacity of an organization arises when colleagues willingly struggle together in a common work that they love. (Wheatley & Kellner-Rogers, 1999)*

Friedman's book *Trying Hard is Not Enough* (2005) gives lots of other examples of where OBA has been used to good effect.

Child-focused

Well-crafted outcome statements speak to us about the children and young people that we came into this work to help. When we take an outcome focus in our partnership work, it helps us to re-connect to our vocation and to keep those children, young people and their families at the forefront of our thinking and our actions.

Our staff crave meaning and authenticity in their work. They simply won't thrive if they are left feeling they are part of some management-led sham that values impressions over substance. Nor will they thrive in meaningless bureaucracy that has no meaning to them or any value to service users. Outcomes help define goals in ways that feel real to us – ways that we feel we can make some personal commitment to. Outcomes reach the parts that tired old mission statements can't.

Concise

Purposes need to be described in ways that are memorable and portable. Wordy, jargon-laden statements of purpose don't have any value in a world where media are competing for our attention. They need to be written in ways that allow us to recall them when we need them. For example, when we're making a difficult decision about a child's future or we're reshaping a service system as a result of financial constraints.

Not surprisingly, the uncompromising tone of outcome statements can make administrators and lawyers feel uncomfortable. However, we need to resist attempts to qualify outcomes with clauses like 'Children are safe, wherever possible' or 'Children and young people achieve their potential within the available budget'.

Constancy of purpose

Outcomes are constant over time and place. This means that they can give us continuity and stability through times of change. This quality is particularly valuable in partnership work where it is unlikely that at any time one of your key partners will be undergoing some sort of structural change or change of personnel. This might come from changes in the ruling political party, funding levels, boundary changes, management-fad, and organisational structure.

Change may be the result of a natural disaster or catastrophe. For example, on 25 June 2007, over 100mm of rain fell on the city of Hull over a 24-hour period. Almost 9000 homes were left under water and many schools, youth clubs and nurseries were severely damaged. We used our outcomes statement to help shape and track our relief and restoration efforts.

Mark Friedman (2005) stresses the need to make a clear distinction between what he calls population accountability and performance accountability:

: **Population accountability** describes the arrangements for holding high-level partnerships (for example, a children's partnership board) collectively responsible for progress towards better outcomes for all children within their jurisdiction.

: **Performance accountability** describes the arrangements for holding service or programme managers responsible for the outcomes that their services are responsible for.

Friedman (2005) makes the point that it's singularly unhelpful to hold a manager of one service responsible for outcomes that can only be improved by the collective and sustained effort of a whole partnership. He comments:

> *This kind of unfair responsibility causes managers to be defensive, closed and narrowly protective of their agencies, precisely the kind of behaviour that works against any chance for real progress.*

Challenging

Outcomes give us a vision of an ideal future state – something that we aspire to, but which will always be beyond our reach.

The next time you have a day set aside for team building, you might want to pay a visit to the Town Hall in Sienna. Here you'll find a set of frescoes collectively called *The Allegory and Effects of Good and Bad Government*. Painted in 12th century by Lorenzetti, the frescoes depict the effects of good and bad government on town and country. Taken together, they create a powerful and enduring visual image for local taxpayers of what good outcomes looked like – and the dire consequences of neglect and corruption in public life.

Like Lorenzetti's images, outcome statements should leave us with a powerful and challenging mental image of the world that we're working to create with children and young people. It's a place that we know will only be reached through long and concerted effort across our partnership.

Leaders will play a significant role in creating and sustaining this effort. Indeed, effective leadership is arguably the single most important factor in making advances towards improving outcomes across a whole population. We can learn a lot by studying the habits of experienced leaders like Nigel Richardson, currently Director of Children's Services in Leeds, England or Con Hogan, former director of Human Services in Vermont, USA, who have both used outcome-led change programmes to good effect. It is noticeable how they work with outcomes statements to build commitment and galvanise action around a common cause. This approach resonates strongly with a social movement perspective of change management where leaders aim to connect people's core personal and professional values to support the change efforts. Such an approach has recently been explored as a way of managing health and healthcare improvements (NHS Institute for Innovation and Improvement, 2009).

Outcome statements should leave us with a powerful and challenging mental image of the world that we're working to create with children and young people

Comprehensive

Outcomes focus on the 'whole child' and not just a part of a child's life. A well-crafted set of outcome statements draws our attention to the interdependence between each outcome domain. When we begin to explore interdependencies in this way, partnership working becomes unavoidable. This can help draw agencies away from the silo mentality that limits and in some cases undermines the collective effectiveness of services and wastes public money.

'Consilience' is another word that I thought about using in this little 'c-word' mnemonic that I'm using here. As you can see, I opted for 'comprehensive' instead. (If mnemonics are devices for helping us remember stuff, I reasoned that it probably wasn't a good idea to include a word that wasn't in everyday use). The word 'consilience' refers to what Edward Wilson (1998) calls the unity of knowledge – "a 'jumping together' of knowledge by the linking of facts and fact-based theory across the disciplines to create a common groundwork of explanation". Anyone that has spent any time working in a partnership will understand the significance of this idea. The outcomes that we talk about are interdependent. For example, for children to achieve their potential they need to be safe, healthy, involved and so on. To make progress, we talk about the need for 'joined-up thinking'. Too often, this ends up looking like 'cut n' paste' thinking, lifting facts and figures from one report or another to create the impression of a coherent whole rather than a unified understanding of 'what works' for children, young people and their carers.

Having people who can form and sustain effective partnerships gives a community a massive advantage. Trusting relationships are usually the place where innovative work begins

There is a simple utility in building trusting relationships across a partnership. Having people who can form and sustain effective partnerships gives a community a massive advantage. Trusting relationships are usually the place where innovative work begins. They also have a massive economic value. At a really basic level, if you trust someone, you don't have to spend time (and therefore money) checking up on them nor do you have to provide a duplicate service because you can't trust them to get their bit right.

I've been fortunate in working with some brilliant people during my career, people whose efforts brought about ground-breaking advances in local services. I've also worked with too many people that Professor Robert Sutton (2007) has a name for and describes in his book *The No Asshole Rule: Building a Civilized Workplace and Surviving One That Isn't*. In the book Sutton describes the damage that bad people do to profits. In partnerships, the damage is to children's lives. Regardless of whether you're working at a casework level or a strategic level, children and their carers are relying on you to get things right for them. Getting things right means having the people skills to build and sustain trusting relationships.

Consensus of purpose

When we set our goals in terms of outcomes, partnerships become unavoidable. Better outcomes can only be achieved by focused and sustained effort across whole communities. Outcomes give partnerships a starting place for building consensus because by their nature they are uncontested. As Friedman (2005) points out, outcomes help us to create some common ground on which we can gather and move forward from. He reminds us that people rarely fall out around 'ends', it is usually 'means' that prove to be more contentious.

Outcome statements can work across different settings and organisational levels. For example, outcomes can be just as useful for shaping a care plan for an individual child as they can a strategic plan that might serve 50,000 children.

Conclusion

Listening to some managers in the public service performance community, you'd think that public services only existed to be measured and inspected ('We're measured therefore we are'). Their enthusiasm for outcomes seems driven by their enthusiasm for measuring things. For me, the ideas of outcome-orientated practices will always be far more important than just measurement – important though it is.

The simple act of agreeing the purposes of our collective efforts in terms of the outcomes we seek to deliver provides a foundation for local partnership working, and for working with individual children. Holding a clear and unwavering picture of the future we are trying to bring about is not only eminently practical, it can sustain us through the adversity that we will inevitably face when we are working for social change.

Outcomes can sustain us. They can give us hope. And hope dies last.[1] ■

REFERENCES

Friedman, M. (2005). *Trying Hard is Not Enough: How to produce measurable improvement for customers and communities*. Victoria: Trafford.

NHS Institute for Innovation and Improvement (2009). *The Power of One, the Power of Many: Bringing social movement thinking to health and healthcare improvement*. Coventry: NHS Institute for Innovation and Improvement.

Pinnock. M. (2011) *A guide to developing an outcome-orientated approach to managing your team*. Sutton, UK: Community Care Inform.

Senge, P. (1990). *The Fifth Discipline: The art and practice of the learning organisation*. New York: Doubleday.

Sutton, R. (2007). *The No Asshole Rule: Building a civilised workplace and surviving one that isn't*. London: Sphere.

Wheatley, M. & Kellner-Rogers, M. (1999). What Do We Measure and Why? Questions About The Uses of Measurement. *Journal for Strategic Performance Measurement*. Available from http://www.margaretwheatley.com/articles/whymeasure.html.

Wilson, E.O. (1998). *Consilience: The Unity of Knowledge*. London: Abacus.

Mike Pinnock has been involved in partnership working for children and young people for the past 38 years both as a practitioner and as a senior manager. In the early Nineties, he was one of the first people in the UK to explore and apply the ideas of outcome-based services for children and their families. Since then he has worked extensively with Mark Friedman of the Fiscal Studies Policies Institute on applying the Outcome-Based Accountability (OBA) framework. He has contributed to a number of national and international projects on outcome-based work. He currently works as an independent researcher/trainer and as a consultant researcher at the Centre for Child and Family Research, Loughborough University. He has written and co-authored a number of publications on outcome-based work and related subjects, the most recent being for the Munro Review of Chid Protection. See: http://www.education.gov.uk/publications/standard/publicationDetail/Page1/CWRC-00079-2011.

He lives with his family in North Lincolnshire.

---

1 The phrase "hope dies last" is borrowed from the title of the book Hope Dies Last: Making a Difference in an Indifferent World by Studs Terkel (2005). It could have just as easily come from the (arguably under-rated) Italian post hardcore rock band which shares the same name.

APPENDIX D (See Chapter 1 Essay 10)

Transforming Life Chances
for Children, Young People and Families in Leeds, UK
Using Outcomes-Based Accountability

Leeds is the third largest city in the UK, with a diverse population of more than 750,000 people, including 180,000 children and young people. It is an affluent and prospering city, but also has some of the most deprived communities in the country. In July 2009, the Office for Standards in Education (Ofsted) carried out an inspection of city services for vulnerable children and young people, as part of an ongoing high-profile national inspection programme. The inspection was extremely critical of services in the city, finding that the city failed to adequately safeguard children and young people. Subsequently the government gave the local council a 'notice to improve' and for a short time established an independently chaired improvement board to guide and support improvements.

In 2010 the council responded by making some significant changes. A new Chief Executive, Tom Riordan and a newly elected Executive Council Member for Children's Services, Councillor Judith Blake, appointed Nigel Richardson as Director of Children's Services. This appointment, along with a new leadership team, acted as the catalyst for a new 'whole system' approach to services for children and young people. From the outset, Outcome based accountability (OBA) was chosen as the means through which the Council and the wider partnership would manage and judge the effect of their collective efforts.

Working with a partnership of key service providers, a new plan for children's services was developed and implemented. This plan centred on creating a single, unifying narrative about the ambition for children in the city: To be the best city in the UK to grow up in, and to be recognised as a Child Friendly City. At the heart of this ambition was an emphasis on

adopting three fundamental behaviours to guide every aspect of work with children and families: The first centred on listening to the voice of the child so that their thoughts and feelings would guide the decisions practitioners make that affect them. The second was about using approaches, techniques and language that works *with* families to solve problems, rather than doing things to them, for them, or not doing anything at all. This restorative approach empowers families to safely and appropriately find their own solutions to the problems they face. The third behaviour was about using OBA to constantly and consistently question whether anyone is better off as a result of the work being done and to shape and improve services accordingly. The combination of these three behaviours, within a whole-system, city-wide approach, has underpinned the improvement journey in Leeds between 2010 and 2015.

The new Children and Young People's (CYP) Plan for the city was designed using OBA principles and practice. Under the Child Friendly City vision, it set out five outcomes and 12 priorities that would guide all work for children, young people and families. It identified the need to relentlessly focus on three areas in particular, referred to as the Leeds three **'obsessions.'** Based on the theory that 'anywhere leads to everywhere', making an impact on these areas would have a positive knock-on effect right across all work with children and families. The three obsessions are:

• Safely and appropriately reducing the need for children to be looked after.
• Reducing the number of young people who are Not in Education, Employment or Training (NEET)
• Improving school attendance

The OBA methodology was used to develop turning the curve 'scorecards' for each of the obsessions. These scorecards have been regularly employed to report progress to the city's Children and Families Trust Board - comprising of senior figures from services working most closely with children and young people. Crucially, the scorecards were used to track the effectiveness of the partnership's collective efforts to 'turn the curve'. The reports made it possible to visualise the difference between the likely course of events based on the historical trajectory (e.g. if the number of children in care had continued to increase in line with past trends), and the impact that the various interventions were having on helping to 'turn the curve' (e.g. the number of children looked after declines from its current level). By using such graphs Leeds was able to show the impact of new initiatives and investment at different times during its improvement journey. The example in Figure D.1 demonstrates this in relation to the number of children in care in Leeds:

Although this approach provided a framework for using OBA to track progress, the bigger challenge for a city as large and diverse as Leeds was implementing and then embedding the outcome-based approach consistently across all of its work, including frontline practice as well as in 'enabling' services such as human resources (HR), information technology (ICT), finance, asset management. To do this, over five years Leeds consistently emphasised an outcome-based approach as one of the three fundamental behaviours that underpinned work with children and families. In addition the city took a number of incremental steps from awareness-raising, through training and then application at a local and city-wide level, to embed OBA across different areas of work.

Leeds has particularly emphasised the use of OBA across local 'clusters' of services. In Leeds clusters are the local partnerships between schools and the other services within a given area that must work together to provide a holistic approach to improving outcomes for children and young people. This includes children's centres, health professionals, youth services, voluntary sector organisations and the police. Local elected members also sit on clusters linked to their ward. In total there are 25 clusters across the city.

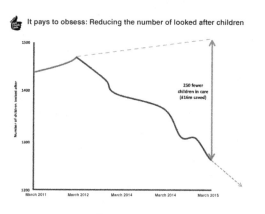

Figure D.1

Each cluster has completed an OBA workshop on each of the three obsessions, drawing together partners to focus on how to make a difference at a local level. OBA has become a key tool for clusters to review and refocus their work. The clusters used OBA as a basis for developing the 'top 100 methodology', identifying those families causing the greatest challenges for service providers in the local area. This has then enabled a more targeted, co-ordinated and consistent approach to multi-agency support for those families.

Across its wider improvement work, Children's Services used OBA to progress a variety of specific projects where a clear impact could be demonstrated. For example:

• OBA was used as the methodology to address school place planning across the city, providing a framework to tackle a shortage of places given a rapidly growing population. Over 1400 additional primary school places have been created through this work.

• An OBA session followed the launch of the custody pathfinder programme (which aims to reduce the need for children to be remanded or sentenced to custody). The actions implemented reduced custody "bednights" by almost one third over 18 months.

• The OBA approach has been used to launch and develop the Families First initiative in Leeds (part of the UK's national troubled families programme). It looked at how to use data and what each partner could bring to the programme. It enabled the programme to progress quickly and with clear focus. Leeds successfully supported all 2500 families involved in the first phase to achieve improved outcomes and was nationally recognised for its approach.

In each case it was the combination of the three Leeds 'behaviours': using an OBA methodology; running events and planning in a way that works restoratively *with* people; and ensuring the voice of children and young people featured strongly in the process; that proved a successful combination for turning talk into action in a way that involved people in decisions that affected them.

OBA was increasingly adopted in Leeds not just by children's services, but as a city-wide approach for any issue where the methodology could help find solutions. In 2014 the city launched a series of high profile 'breakthrough' projects - on issues such as housing need, city

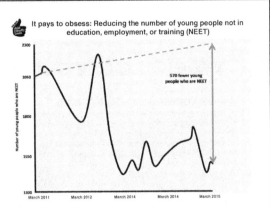

Figure D.2

centre improvement, domestic violence and healthy living. These cross-cutting projects were intended to bring multi-agency partners together to concentrate attention on some of the most difficult issues facing the city. In each case an OBA launch session and methodology was used to drive the planning and development of this work and ensure consistency of approach across different partners.

With OBA established as a city-wide approach, Leeds Children's Services sought to broaden ownership of the feedback data it generated right across the city, to ensure everyone could see how their work was contributing to a collective effort to address the biggest priorities. This work is best demonstrated by the use of a weekly 'Obsessions progress tracker', (see the example shown below). It was produced in a format that enabled all staff/partners to quickly see the difference their collective contributions were making.

The tracker, which became known in Leeds as the 'Thing of Beauty,' arrived weekly in people's inbox and was used in various meeting agendas to inform key discussions and debates about the three OBA performance questions - *How much did we do? How well did we do it? Is anybody better off?* Leeds also broke this data down to a 'cluster' level. This enabled city-wide *and* local performance data to be considered against the three obsessions so that action could be taken quickly to target areas where progress

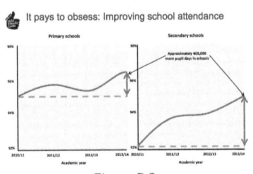

Figure D.3

was lagging. Mike Pinnock, who has been involved in the introduction and development of OBA in Leeds, emphasised that the tracker was an example of how feedback data could be used to engage and energise staff across the partnership, "We deliberately chose a graphical format that people would associate with the sorts of data they use in their daily lives - like a weather report or a stock market index. The intention was to bring some

Weekly obsessions tracker

Week commencing 16 November 2015

Obsession	Latest position this week	Change since last week	Change since CYPP start	Percentage change since CYPP start	Progress since CYPP start
Safely reduce the number of children looked after	1251	-5	-179	-12.5	
Reduce the number of young people not in employment, education or training (NEET)	1389	0	-390	-18.6	
Reduce school absence: primary	3.9	-0.1	-2.0	n/a	
Reduce school absence: secondary	5.3	0.3	-2.2	n/a	

Produced by Children's Performance Service
More information is available on the Leeds Observatory
observatory.leeds.gov.uk

Leeds
CITY COUNCIL

Figure D.4

focus and immediacy to the partnership's efforts. Like a weather report, the primary role of the weekly "Thing of Beauty" was to keep people's attention on something that was important - not to explain it".

In January 2015, the Ofsted inspectors returned to Leeds and found a transformed service. Between 2011 and 2015, the number of looked after children had safely and appropriately reduced from 1,450 to less than 1,300. Primary school attendance and secondary school attendance increased by 2% and 2.2% respectively. The number of young people not in education employment or training declined by nearly 500 (a 22% decline). The Inspector's final report stated... 'The application of the outcomes based accountability approach... is facilitating a shared understanding of priorities for children... (and) the 'three obsessions' are providing a sharp focus for strategic and operational thinking'. The inspectors rated the services as 'good' overall and 'outstanding' for leadership, management and governance, the highest rating available for the strand, which incorporates performance management.

Appendix E (See Chapter 1 Essay 14)

TOOL FOR CHOOSING A COMMON LANGUAGE

Ideas	Possible Labels (and modifiers)	Choice
A. THE BASICS		
1. A system or process for holding people in a geographic area responsible for the well-being of the total population or a defined subpopulation.	Population Accountability	
2. A system or process for holding managers and workers responsible for the performance of their programs, agencies and service systems.	Performance Accountability	
3. A condition of well-being for children, adults, families and communities.	Result, Outcome, Goal (Population, Community-wide)	
4. A measure that helps quantify the achievement of a population result.	Indicator, Benchmark (Population, Community-wide)	
5. A measure of how well a program, agency or service system is working.	Performance measure, Performance indicator	
6. A measure of the quantity of effort (how much service was delivered).	How much did we do?, Quantity of effort, Inputs, Outputs	
7. A measure of the quality of effort (how well the service functions were performed).	How well did we do it?, Quality of effort, Efficiency measure, Process measure	
8. A measure of the quantity and quality of effect on customers' lives. (Note: for infrastructure, effect on condition of infrastructure.)	Is anyone better off?, Is anyone or anything improved?, Customer result or outcome, Quantity & Quality of effect	
9. A visual display of the history and forecast(s) for a measure.	Baseline, Trendline	
10. Doing better than the forecast part of the baseline.	Turning the curve, Beating the baseline	

TOOL FOR CHOOSING A COMMON LANGUAGE (continued)

Ideas	Possible Labels (and modifiers)	Choice
B. OTHER IMPORTANT IDEAS		
1. A picture of a desired future that is hard but possible to attain.	Vision, Desired future	
2. The purpose of an organization.	Mission, Purpose	
3. A person (organization or entity) who directly benefits from service delivery. (generic category)	Customer, Client, Consumer, Beneficiary, Service user	
4. A person (or organization) with a significant interest in the performance of a program, agency or service system or population quality of life effort.	Stakeholder, Constituent	
5. A person (or organization) with a role to play in achieving desired ends.	Partner (Current, Potential, Active, Inactive)	
6. An analysis of causes and conditions that helps explain why a baseline looks the way it does.	Story behind the baseline, Root cause analysis	
7. Possible actions that could have a positive effect on a population indicator or performance measure.	What works, Options	
8. A coherent set of actions that has a reasoned chance of producing a desired effect.	Strategy	
9. A description of proposed actions.	Action Plan, Strategic plan	
10. The components of an action or strategic plan.	Goals & Objectives, Planned actions	
11. A description of why we think an action or set of actions will work.	Theory of change (Logic model)	
12. A prioritized list of where we need new or better data.	Data Development Agenda	
13. A prioritized list of where we need new information/research about causes and solutions.	Information & Research Agenda	
14. A desired future level of achievement for a population indicator or performance measure.	Target, Goal, Standard, Benchmark	
15. A study or analysis of how well a program is working or has worked.	Program evaluation, Performance evaluation	

(Other modifiers: measurable, urgent, priority, targeted, incremental, systemic, core, quantitative, qualitative, intermediate, ultimate short-term, mid-term, long-term, internal, external, infernal, eternal, allegorical, extraterrestrial)   **FPSI revised Nov 2013**

Appendix F (See Chapter 1 Essay 27)

RBA and Mental Models

Old Mental Models	RBA Mental Models
1. Data is something used against us.	1. We can use data for our own purposes. (the democratization of data)
2. Services solve the problems of people and communities.	2. Services help people and communities solve their own problems.
3. It is fair to hold a department of government responsible for solving a social problem (e.g. Dept of Mental Health solves mental illness; Child Protection solves child abuse).	3. Social problems are matters of Population Accountability and are the shared responsibility of many partners across the community.
4. A Planning framework can't be any good if it's not complicated.	4. Simple frameworks like RBA can be powerful. Simple planning "containers" can hold complex content.
5. I can't change anything.	5. I can be a leader.
6. The future is shaped by others.	6. The future is shaped by me.
7. Data is about precise measurement.	7. Data is about approximation.
8. We can understand cause and effect if we study it hard enough.	8. Cause and effects are rarely simple. Think contribution not attribution.
9. All important actions cost money.	9. Much can be accomplished with no-cost and low-cost actions.
10. Experts know more than I do about my work.	10. I am an expert.
11. Outside evaluation is the only way to tell if our program is working.	11. We can evaluate our own work.
12. Improvement is when we meet our targets.	12. Improvement is turning the curve on important population indicators and performance measures.
13. There is a long list of performance measurement categories.	13. All performance measures can fit into three categories: How much did we do? How well did we do it? Is anyone better off?
14. Clear language is impossible. Jargon is unavoidable. We can work around language confusion.	14. Clear language and language discipline are both possible and necessary.

RBA and Mental Models (continued)

Old Mental Models	RBA Mental Models
15. Funders are overlords and grantees are serfs.	15. Funders and grantees are partners in improving results/outcomes for customers and communities. (See Next Generation Contracting.)
16. We need permission.	16. We can just do it. Better to ask for forgiveness than permission.
17. People eventually burn out.	17. People get disconnected from purpose and can be rejuvenated by reconnecting to purpose. Program purpose is embodied in Is anyone better off? measures.
18. Don't change horses in mid stream.	18. We are always in mid stream. Change when you need to.
19. Solutions can be stable.	19. There is no such thing as a steady state. If you're not getting better you're getting worse.
20. In times of cutbacks, hunker down, scale back, lower expectations.	20. In times of cutbacks, reconnect to purpose, reconnect to partners, find opportunities, find new ways of doing things.
21. Exclusive processes and secrets are necessary for self defense.	21. The real power lies in inclusion, transparent processes, and shared purpose.
22. Diversity is a problem.	22. Diversity is a strength.
23. Differences of opinion are a problem.	23. Differences of opinion are healthy in the context of shared purpose.
24. Management, budgeting, and strategic planning, are 3 separate systems.	24. Management, budgeting, and strategic planning, are 3 parts of a single system.
25. The first thing you do is a mission statement.	25. Mission statements can come after development and use of performance measures.
26. It takes months of planning before anything can actually be done.	26. You can get from talk to action in one hour.
27. We start by analyzing what is wrong and then trying to fix it.	27. We start by defining the desired end state in terms of results/outcomes and then move toward it.
28. We need targets to motivate people and organizations to perform well.	28. Targets are OK if they are fair and useful, and if they produce aspirational behavior, not fear of punishment or game playing.

Appendix G (See Chapter 1 Essay 28 for scoring methods)

RBA Implementation Self Assessment
for Government and Nonprofit Organizations

1. Language Discipline (10)

  a. Has your group or organization adopted a common language using the Tool for Choosing a Common Language or some other method? Does this common language allow you to clearly distinguish population and performance accountability? (7)
  b. Can you crosswalk your language usage to that of your funders and other partners? (3)

2. Population Accountability (30)

  a. Has your organization identified one or more population level results or conditions of well-being stated in plain language to which your work contributes? (5)
  b. Have you identified the 3 to 5 most important indicators for each of these results? (5)
  c. Have you created a baseline with history and a forecast for each of these measures? (5)
  d. Have you analyzed the story behind these baselines? (5)
  e. Do you have a written analysis of what it would take to turn these conditions around at the national, state, county, city or community level? (5)
  f. Have you articulated the role your organization plays in such a strategy? (5)

3. Performance Accountability (45)

  a. Has your organization established the 3 to 5 most important performance measures for what you do, using the performance accountability categories *How much did we do? How well did we do it? Is anyone better off?* (5)
  b. Have you created a baseline with history and a forecast for each of these measures? (5)
  c. Do you track these measures on a daily, weekly, monthly or quarterly basis? (10)
  d. Do you periodically review how you are doing on these measures and develop action plans to do better using the performance accountability 7 questions? (10)
  e. Have you adapted your management, budget, strategic planning, grant application, and progress reporting forms and formats to reflect systematic thinking about your contribution to population conditions and your organization's performance? (5)
  f. Are the population and performance baseline curves you are trying to turn displayed prominently as one or more charts on the wall? (5)
  g. Have you identified an in-house expert to train and coach other staff in this work? (5)

4. Bottom line Quality of Service (15)

  a. Considering case mix difficulty, are you doing well or poorly on the most important *Is Anyone Better off?* measures compared to others? (Others = comparable providers, industry benchmarks, or reasonable targets or standards) (5)
  b. How are you doing on the most important *How well did we do it?* measures compared to others? (Others = comparable providers, industry benchmarks, or reasonable targets or standards) (5)
  c. Have you turned any curves? (5)

5. Bonuses and Penalties (-20 to +10)

  a. Research and Evaluation Bonus: Do you have (recent i.e. less than 3 to 5 yrs. old) research or evaluation evidence that shows your services cause improvement in customers' lives as shown by *Is Anyone Better off?* measures? Yes = plus 10 No = 0
  b. Skimming Penalty: Is there any evidence that you are skimming easy customers in order to increase success rates on *Is Anyone Better off?* measures? Yes = minus 10 No = 0
  c. Unit Cost Penalty: Given the intensity of your services are your unit costs per customer in line with other providers in the field? Yes = 0 No = minus 10

Appendix H (See Chapter 2 Essay 2)

FPSI FISCAL POLICY STUDIES INSTITUTE

7 Avenida Vista Grande #140 Santa Fe NM 87508

COLLECTIVE IMPACT USING RBA

Collective Impact and RBA are a perfect fit. The idea of working together to produce community "impact" is at the heart of both bodies of work. And RBA complements Collective Impact in other ways. Collective Impact literature sets out conditions for the success of community change efforts, and RBA provides specific methods to help partners meet those conditions. More and more places are describing their work in terms of implementing Collective Impact using RBA. The following summary addresses how communities can use RBA to meet the five conditions for Collective Impact set out by John Kania and Mark Kramer in their article *Collective Impact, Stanford Social Innovation Review* (Winter 2011).

Condition 1) A common agenda: Since Collective Impact is principally about community or population-level change, the idea of a Collective Impact agenda is first and foremost about population quality of life ambitions the community hopes to achieve. RBA provides a way to articulate such ambitions (or population results) such as "All children are born healthy. All children are ready for school. All families are safe and supportive. A clean and sustainable environment. A prosperous and inclusive economy." For each population result, RBA provides a method to select the most important indicators that tell us the extent to which a given population result is being achieved, e.g. the percentage of low birth-weight births. These measures are displayed as baselines with history and forecast, with success defined as "turning the curve." A Collective Impact agenda can address both population results and the priority indicator curves to turn. (A second meaning for agenda has to do with the idea of an action agenda, addressed below under "mutually reinforcing activities.")

Key Points:
a. RBA provides clarity about the difference between improving population quality of life and improving program performance.
b. Collective Impact agendas can take the form of priority population results (e.g. All children born healthy) and priority indicator curves to turn (e.g. percentage of low birth-weight births).

Condition 2) Shared measurement system: Measurement systems are needed at both the population and performance levels. RBA provides a way to categorize meas-

124

ures into population indicators and three types of performance measures (*How much did we do? How well did we do it? Is anyone better off?*). RBA also provides a method for setting measurement priorities in the form of a three part list: 3 to 5 Headline measures (the best of what we currently have data for), Secondary measures (all other measures for which we have data), and a Data Development Agenda (a prioritized list of where we need new or better data). Population and performance measurement systems should be shared with the community on line. The Results Scorecard provides a tool for managing such complex data sets across communities and across partner organizations. This in turn allows for the creation of a community progress report on quality of life and the development of concise performance reports for programs.

Key Points:
a. RBA provides methods for identifying measurement priorities at both the population and performance levels.
b. These priorities can be used to create a population quality of life report card and program performance reports.
c. The Data Development Agenda allows partners to get new and better data over time.

Condition 3) Mutually reinforcing activities: Change is only possible at the community level if the partners are all pulling in the same direction. This involves agreement on strategies that will have the greatest impact, and action plans to make those strategies a reality. The RBA Turn the Curve process provides a readily understandable process for creating strategies and developing action plans. This process progresses from ends to means through 7 Questions that vary slightly for Population and Performance Accountability. (The 7 Population Accountability questions are shown at right.) The simplest version of this process, the Turn the Curve Exercise, can be completed in one hour. This way of thinking provides a structure for systematically improving strategies and action plans over time. RBA also encourages groups to go beyond planning for incremental change to the more challenging "what would it take?" questions,

---

The 7 Population Accountability Questions

1. What are the quality of life conditions we want for the children, adults and families who live in our community?

2. What would these conditions look like if we could see them?

3. How can we measure these conditions?

4. How are we doing on the most important of these measures?

5. Who are the partners that have a role to play in doing better?

6. What works to do better, including no-cost and low-cost ideas?

7. What do we propose to do?

such as "What would it take for ALL children to succeed in school?" (See the work of Geoffrey Canada.)

Key Points:
a. RBA provides a method for creating strategies and action plans.
b. This allows partners to see how their actions can work together to create impact/improvement on important population results and indicators
c. RBA encourages partnerships to go beyond incremental change to consider "what would it take?" questions.

Condition 4) Continuous communication: The very definition of communication is about understanding what others are saying. Yet, the history of this work, at both the population and performance levels, is one of jargon and confusion. RBA uses plain language descriptions of the core ideas necessary to turn curves. RBA encourages the disciplined use of this language by all partners, enabling them to work together more effectively. And RBA methods promote get-to-the-point communications that are more likely to be read and used.

Key Points:
a. RBA uses plain language descriptions of core ideas to replace current confusing jargon.
b. The disciplined use of RBA common language enables partners to work together more effectively.
c. RBA language discipline, with Turn the Curve thinking, provides a structure for communication that will be understood and used.

Condition 5) Backbone support organization(s): Community level or population level change requires support for functions that span across traditional organizational boundaries. Support can be lodged in a single organization or shared by multiple organizations provided that all necessary functions are covered. RBA can help identify the cross-community functions that require organizational support, including staffing the partnership, managing measurement systems, publishing reports, and keeping track of plans and action commitments. A designated support organization can also serve to facilitate "neutral" Turn the Curve conversations for community partners.

Key Points:
a. RBA can help identify cross-community functions that require special organizational support.
b. RBA can be used to make the case for funding the partnership's plans and the organizational capacity necessary to support effective working together.

For more information see "Achieving 'Collective Impact' with Results-Based Accountability™," Deitre Epps, Results Leadership Group, 2011 (available on resultsaccountability.com and resultsleadership.org)

April, 2014 rev May 2015

APPENDIX I (See Chapter 3 Essay 7)

FPSI FISCAL POLICY STUDIES INSTITUTE

7 Avenida Vista Grande #140 Santa Fe NM 87508

NEXT GENERATION CONTRACTING
A Contract Reform Agenda for Funders and Nonprofits

FPSI produces occasional papers on subjects related to accountability in general and Results-Based Accountability™ (RBA) in particular. This paper responds to requests over the years for ideas about how RBA can be applied to the methods by which government agencies and private philanthropies write agreements with those to whom they give money (referred to here as contractors or grantees).

Following are 10 provisions that I believe should be in contracts of the future.

Provision 1: Specify the 3 to 5 most important performance measures (from the *How well did we do it?* and *Is anyone better off? categories).*

Contracts of the future should specify the top measures to be used in performance reporting and continuous improvement. These should be taken from the *How well did we do it?* and *Is anyone better off?* categories. The choice of measures should be **negotiated** between the funder and the contractor/grantee.

Provision 2: Specify that the contractor will use a continuous improvement process (the RBA 7 Questions).

The contract should specify that the contractor will use some form of continuous improvement process. The RBA 7 Performance Accountability questions are a good choice for this purpose, but if you have something you like better that's OK. Continuous improvement should be used at (or phased in to) every level of the organization.

Provision 3: Specify how the funder and contractor will work in partnership to maximize *Is anyone better off? customer results.*

Right now the relationship between funders and grantees is often a feudal relationship: overlord and serf. Funders can sit back and watch their grantees struggle and it's not their fault. We need to create a more co-equal relationship between funders and grantees, so that they work in partnership to produce the best possible results for their customers. Contracts should specify how this partnership will work, possibly through meetings two, three or four times a year using the 7 Performance Accountability questions as the agenda. At these meetings, funders must be willing to take on tasks to help the contractor/grantee improve.

Provision 4: Specify that the funder will work with the rest of the funding community to simplify and standardize contracting and performance reporting.

If you run a nonprofit anywhere in the world, you probably receive funding from 10 or more funders all with different grant application and performance reporting requirements. You spend all your time running around meeting all these separate requirements and don't have time to do your real job of running the agency. I believe funders have an obligation to get their act together. And this means standardizing application, contracting and reporting requirements. Funders should commit **in writing**, in the contract, to working with other funders toward this end.

Simplification of performance reporting should make use of one page reports. These should include the name and brief description of the program or project and its contribution to population quality of life, the presentation of the three to five most important performance measures in baseline form, the story behind those baselines (including accomplishments), partners with a role to play and the action plan to get better. Attached to each report should be a story about a customer who is better off.

Provision 5: Clear articulation of the role of the contractor/grantee in population/community well-being using the language of contribution and not attribution.

Contracts of the future should explain the role that the contractor's services play in population/community quality of life. Contracts should use the language of contribution, not attribution or proof of impact.

Provision 6: 10% for quality management and administration.

Many contracts with nonprofits provide money for services only and nothing for administration. We have been steadily degrading the infrastructure of the nonprofit community for the past 30 years or more. If we are going to rebuild this essential capacity, we must begin providing set-asides for this purpose in all contracts. 10% is a placeholder. The actual amount may be more or less depending on the size and type of the contract.

Provision 7: Multi-year funding using 3 year rolling contracts

Most funders run funding and contracting processes on an annual basis. Let's say it's a January to December cycle. Somewhere around September each year, you're not sure if you're going to get a contract for the next year. Some of your staff start looking for other jobs. The uncertainty interferes with the delivery of service. Under this system, every year, we **systematically destabilize** the entire nonprofit sector. It needs to stop. When we know we're going to have an on-going relationship with a given organization, why not write a three year rolling contract? After the first year, write a new third year. After each year you write a new third year. You always have a three year contract. Naturally there must be safeguards that allow for termination when necessary, and provisions that allow the amount of the contract to change. But the basic structure of the relationship does not have to be re-established from scratch every year.

Provision 8: Targets that are fair and useful.

There is a long history of overusing and misusing targets. We set unrealistic targets and then beat people up for not meeting them. It's a lousy way to manage. We need to step back and re-assess how we use targets. Targets should meet two criteria. They are fair and useful. Most targets are neither fair nor useful. They're not fair because they're not achievable. And they're not useful because they lead to game playing behavior. What we want from targets is aspirational striving behavior and not games. It is actually not necessary to set targets at all. The idea of turning the curve is a powerful way of gauging progress without ever setting a target. But if you do use targets, make sure they are fair and useful.

Provision 9: Fund flexibility allowing the transfer of up to 10% across line items and across program lines.

Budgets are always approximations. Contractors need flexibility in the administration of the contract. Contracts of the future should allow contractors to move up to 10% (or another specified amount) of the funding between line items and between services without going back to the funder for approval.

Provision 10: Request for Results: Getting past the sometimes negative effects of competitive RFP contracting or tendering.

Current RFP / tendering processes lead to nonprofits competing with each other for grants. These organizations are natural partners, and yet the RFP process turns them into adversaries. Why not try something that Placer County California once did? They had a sizable amount of money they were going to spend to improve specific child, family and community outcomes. They knew exactly which nonprofits were most likely going to get the money. They got them all in the room together — over three 5-hour open space sessions —and let them work together to come up with joint proposals about how best to use the money.

Initial drafts 2008, 2013.

APPENDIX J. (See Chapter 3 Essay 10)

THE CARDIFF AND VALE EXPERIENCE

The Cardiff Chronic Conditions Management Demonstrator

The delivery of co-ordinated, comprehensive and consistent Chronic Conditions Management (CCM) services in the community is an integral part of effective mainstream service delivery in the community. This is a key Ministerial priority, the basis of which was drawn from international evidence and published in *Improving Health and the Management of Chronic Conditions in Wales: an Integrated Model and Framework for Action* (WAG).

Improving CCM across Wales depends on good integrated planning and management in partnership with all stakeholders. The aim of the strategy was to improve health and well-being and reduce the incidence and impact of chronic conditions and the inherent inequalities that exist across Wales.

To help deliver and drive improvements in CCM across Wales in an action centred way, three large scale Service Improvement Demonstrator Projects were established, one in Cardiff, one in north Wales and one in Carmarthenshire. This provided an opportunity to focus effort, support and resources in localities to test and learn from concerted effort across organisational and professional boundaries. Lessons and practical solutions were worked through and used to develop the business case for change which supported further mainstreaming across Wales. The aim of this was to;

> *"Provide and test a sustainable, affordable generic CCM service model that supported patients' needs locally and promoted independent living within the community in order to communicate and inform service change across Wales"*

The Cardiff CCM demonstrator was tasked with establishing how Results Based Accountability (RBA) could be used to drive and support implementation of the CCM strategy to ensure services deliver on meaningful outcomes for the population.

CASE STUDY 1.
RESULTS BASED ACCOUNTABILITY AND THE WELSH EPILEPSY UNIT

The Welsh Epilepsy Unit is a tertiary referral centre for specialist epilepsy services in south Wales. The immediate catchment population covered is 700,000 but many referrals are also taken from elsewhere in Wales. The unit offers a multi-disciplinary approach to epilepsy care and offers a very broad range of services to people with epilepsy, their family and carers.

Getting Started with RBA

In the summer of 2009 a multi-agency steering group was formed to develop and test service improvement opportunities in line with the Epilepsy Service Development Directive (3). One of the core objectives of the group was to establish an RBA framework for monitoring performance and evaluation of epilepsy service improvement. Prior to undertaking any RBA training or workshops a comprehensive service mapping exercise was carried out to ensure the steering group had a common understanding of the gaps in current service provision.

Support was provided by Richard Morton from the Partnership Support Unit (PSU) in the Welsh Local Government Association (WLGA) to deliver an introduction to RBA session to steering group members. Following this session, trainers were trained within the Health Board and all further training and facilitation was carried out internally by the author (CCM Demonstrator Project Lead for Cardiff).

Following discussion it was clear that performance accountability was appropriate. Discussions then focussed on whether the epilepsy "customer group" should be divided to ensure that the needs of patients at different points along the care pathway were met. Using information from the service mapping and gap analysis exercise members of the steering group determined that the group should be split and that "patients with a first suspected seizure or unexplained blackout" would be the customer group for the first RBA exercise.

The Process
A facilitated session was held with the steering group to work through the 7 performance accountability questions for this customer group. Participants completed up to question 6 of the exercise during the 2 hour workshop. A number of tasks were identified regarding the collection and baselining of information and an action plan (question 7) was developed at a further meeting.

The 7 question process for performance accountability was repeated at 2 hour facilitated sessions for other customer groups within the epilepsy service:
- Women taking medication for epilepsy between the ages of 14 – 45 who may become or who are pregnant
- People who are admitted to hospital as a result of a presumed seizure

A further introduction to RBA session was held when new partners joined the group after 6 months. The introduction session followed the same format as the original session.

A report card (Appendix ?) was developed for each of the epilepsy customer groups. Data for these report cards are monitored by the steering group on a monthly basis. All of the Epilepsy report cards and details of the epilepsy developments are available at www.ccmdemonstrators.com.

Benefits and Outcomes
Curves have been turned for the first customer group. Preliminary outcomes include:
- The average length of time from seizure to a confirmed diagnosis has decreased by 81 days from 111 days to 30 days
- The number of patients who have been seen by a specialist within the NICE guideline of two weeks has increased from 35% to 61%
- The average waiting time to see a specialist has decreased from 22 days to 11 days
- The number of admissions following a seizure have decreased from 5 a month to 2 a month on average

Other benefits that have been observed include:
- All stakeholders are fully engaged and have ownership of the service
- The team have felt committed and empowered to drive service development
- Performance management is now positively viewed by the team as a tool to enable improvement
- The development of a clear line of sight between Board and LSB priorities and patient outcomes at a departmental level

Challenges

Challenges experienced by the team included:

- Knowing how to start the process was difficult and needed support from the PSU e.g. 'how long does it take?', 'who needs to be in the room?' etc.
- The lack of availability of patient outcome data was an issue. During the process the performance measures chosen were changed to enable meaningful data collection.
- Whether partners that joined the group mid-process needed "training" in RBA. One additional training session was undertaken as described above but partners joining later on have not had access to this.

Next Steps

The Epilepsy Steering Group continue to collect and monitor data for the performance measures and develop the agreed actions.

April 2007 - April 2010 (Monthly)

Chronic Conditions Management Demonstrator
Arddangoswyt Rheoli Cyflyrau Cronig
CARDIFF | CAERDYDD

GIG
NHS

THE WELSH EPILEPSY UNIT
Service Description: The Welsh Epilepsy Unit is a tertiary referral centre for specialist epilepsy services in South Wales. The immediate catchment population covered s 700,000 but many referrals are also taken from elsewhere in Wales. The Unit offers a multidisciplinary approach to epilepsy care and offers a very broad range of services to people with epilepsy, their families and carers.

DEFINED SERVICE USERS: Patients with a first suspected seizure or unexplained blackout

HEADLINE PERFORMANCE MEASURES
1. % seen by a specialist within 2 weeks (NICE guideline)
2. No. admissions to hospital for a seizure
3. Average waiting time to see a specialist
4. % did not attend (DNA) first seizure clinic

HOW ARE WE DOING?

% Seen by a Specialist within 2 Weeks

No. Admissions for a Seizure

STORY BEHIND THE BASELINE
Limited clinic capacity with unpredictable demand
Small team – unable to cover absence to prevent clinic cancellation
Low frequency of clinics causing delay if appointment not suitable for the patient
Clinic booked by Epilepsy Unit admin staff – if admin staff on leave the clinic slots are not filled
Consultant triage's fax referrals – delay if unavailable
Patient anxiety and concern re implications of a diagnosis e.g. driving
Stigma attached to Epilepsy
Patients put off by unit name – diagnosis seems pre-determined
Nurses unable to refer for EEG leading to delay in diagnostics and confirmed diagnosis
New nurse led emergency unit assessment service for first seizure patients has improved performance measures but out of hours service reverts to old pathway
Primary Care does not have fast track access for first seizure clinics
Primary Care are not made aware if a patient DNA's so can't follow up

DATA DEVELOPMENT AGENDA
1. Seizure frequency
2. Death rate
3. % prescribed incorrect medication
4. % who report they feel satisfied or better off

Average Waiting Time to See a Specialist

DNA Rate

PARTNERS WHO CAN HELP US
Emergency Unit, Radiology, Neurophysiology, Medical Records, A&C staff, Consultants, Specialist Nurses, Ambulance Trust, Cardiology, Psychology, Care of the Elderly, Neurosurgery, Prison, Voluntary Sector, Practice Nurses, GP's, Family members/witnesses, Drug & Alcohol Services, Occupational Health, Referral Management Centre, Obstetrics, Management, Communications Department, Patients

WHAT ARE WE GOING TO DO TO DO TO IMPROVE PERFORMANCE?
1. Change the name of the "Epilepsy Unit" to the "Alan Richens Unit"
2. Develop nurse led first seizure clinics to cover when Consultants unavailable
3. Develop dedicated fast track clinic for Primary Care referrals
4. Enable specialist nurse referral for EEG
5. Develop process to inform Primary Care of DNA

APPENDIX K (See Chapter 3 Essay 12)

Additional Notes on Teacher Performance Evaluation

The research of W. L. Sanders and The Tennessee Value-Added System (TVAAS) is often cited as justification for using student achievement test scores in high-stakes individual teacher evaluation. I believe these methods and the research behind them are flawed, and here's why.

Sanders' research shows that teacher quality affects student achievement test scores[24] (a finding that borders on tautology). However, Sanders' research findings do **not** support the use of achievement test data to score and compare **individual** teacher's performance.

The question is a narrow one: Can you construct a valid and reliable teacher performance score from achievement test data alone? There are actually some easy ways to investigate this question. Here are three simple readily testable hypotheses, and three thought experiments.

Experiment #1 (testing reliability). Take the top 5 performing teachers in year 1 and put them all in the poorest performing schools in year 2. Compare their teacher evaluation score using only achievement test data. Hypothesis: The same teachers will receive significantly worse scores in year 2 than year 1.

Experiment #2 (testing validity). Take the teacher scores derived from achievement test data alone and see if it correlates with teacher scores from other sources (classroom observation, peer review, parent and student feedback etc.). Hypothesis. The correlation is weak at best.

Experiment #3. Take the teachers for whom there is the greatest disparity in Experiment #2. Follow what happens to them in the year after they are given their evaluation score. Hypothesis. The unreliable (unfair) teacher evaluations (derived from achievement test score components) are driving good teachers (as judged by non-achievement test data) out of poor schools and out of the teaching profession entirely.

If this last hypothesis is correct, this means that achievement test score construction for individual teachers is having the EXACT OPPOSITE EFFECT of what we seek to

---

[24] "Wright, Horn, and Sanders (WHS, 1997) conclude that teachers are the most important factor affecting student learning. "Evaluating value-added models for teacher accountability," Dan McCaffrey ... [et al.], Rand Corporation, 2003"

achieve: good teachers in every classroom. Continued use of this methodology will exacerbate the disparity of teaching quality between wealthy and poor schools, and will drain the education system of badly needed talent.

Thought Experiment #1: Imagine a class where the five best students leave during the year. Test scores may actually go down from the class beginning average to the class ending average. Did the teacher get worse because the best students left?

Looking at the TVAAS methodology (www.tn.gov/education/data/TVAAS.shtml), even if the leaving and entering students are excluded from the rating, the teacher is still disadvantaged by the measurement of growth only for the less able students. There are numerous other aspects of the TVAAS methodology that are open to challenge. For example, the use of a normal curve to calculate actual vs. expected growth means that students who achieve more growth than expected must (generally) be offset by students who achieve less. (Consider the anomalous situation where every student achieved a lower test score than the previous year, but, because of the effects of the normal distribution curve on their expected rank relative to their peers, approximately half of these students (the ones who declined the least) would show expected or greater than expected "growth"!! Has anyone argued this point? Purely from the standpoint of mathematics - and I was a math major ("Always check the end points.") - this makes the entire score construction methodology highly suspect.

Thought Experiment # 2: Can you tell me, using achievement test score data alone, who are the 5 best and 5 worst school superintendents in your state? Does this ranking correlate with what else is known about their performance?

Thought Experiment #3 (exercise for a group of secondary school students): Get together 4 or 5 students in a study group. Pose this question: Teacher A and Teacher B are both 3rd grade teachers. The school computes the amount of increase in reading scores from the beginning of the year to the end of the year for each class. Teacher A's class scores increased by 1.1 grade levels. Teacher B's class scores increased by .85 grade level. Is this enough information by itself to conclude that Teacher A is better than Teacher B? Why or why not? The primary customers of the education system might have some insight into the validity of using data this way.

There are a few more interesting things to say about Sanders' research. Sanders developed the Tennessee Value-Added Assessment System (TVAAS), and the Educational Value-Added Assessment System (EVAAS), as a method for measuring a teacher's effect on student performance [now here's the important part] "by tracking the progress of students against themselves over the course of their school career with their assignment to various teachers' classes."

If I read this right, it means that for any given student, some teachers "produced" more or less achievement gains over the course of the student's "career." What is clever (and arguably deceptive) about this research design and its principal finding is that it purports to control for degree of difficulty by tracking the same student over different years. This ASSUMES that an individual student maintains the same "degree of difficulty" over time, and we know that this is not true. A student's personality, ability , home circumstance and many other factors combine to make a student "easier" or "harder" to teach in any given year, and, for that matter, on any given day. The use of the same student does NOT control for degree of difficulty, and therefore achievement gains ARE NOT comparable from teacher to teacher. Even if this assumption could be granted for an individual student, it is not relevant to, nor does it begin to address, the difference in degree of difficulty of whole classrooms, the basis on which current teacher performance scores are calculated.

Finally, for now, I was unable to find any discussion of margin of error on the Tennessee site. The VAM methodology might produce some interesting research data for a large sample, but any data at the level of the individual student or individual teacher must have a very large margin of error that makes it inappropriate for high stakes use.

I am not saying that achievement test scores are unreliable. They are very useful at the level of school improvement planning. Even the TVAAS growth scores might be useful at this level. Nor am I disagreeing with the conclusion of the Rand authors when they say,

We conclude that although the papers all have shortcomings, together they provide evidence that teachers have discernable, differential effects on student achievement, and that these effects appear to persist into the future.
(p. xiii)

What I am saying is that there is no way to construct a valid and reliable score for individual teacher performance from achievement test score data or growth data alone. And if the achievement test score/growth portion of the overall teacher's score is invalid and unreliable, then the overall evaluation score is also invalid and unreliable.

Imagine you are baking a cake. You assemble 9 of the usual healthy ingredients (eggs, flour, milk etc.) and then add a 10th ingredient, rat poison. Even though 9 of 10 ingredients are healthy the overall cake is still toxic. If you bake a teacher evaluation and 4 of 5 criteria are fair but one is unfair, then the overall evaluation will be unfair (and maybe toxic).

FPSI Draft 10/2/14

Appendix L (See Chapter 3 Essay 22)

MEASURING ALIGNMENT OF GROUP CHARACTERISTICS

What method can be used to precisely measure the alignment between different group distributions? In Juvenile justice, there is a long history of the overrepresentation of minorities among delinquent and incarcerated populations. In Special Education, there are problems of both over-representation and under-representation. It is arguable that African American children are too readily diagnosed with disabilities, and Native American children are too rarely diagnosed. In affirmative action, we look at the distribution of employees by race, gender and ethnicity compared to the population in our community, city, county or state. For community colleges, there is an interest in assuring that the distribution of faculty comports with the population distribution of the communities they serve.

There is a method for measuring this kind of alignment that reduces the differences between two groups to a single number between 0 (complete misalignment) and 100 (perfect alignment).

The differences between each category are added together. This total is divided

Method for Calculating the Degree of Alignment
Between Different Group Distributions
by Race, Ethnicity or Other Characteristics

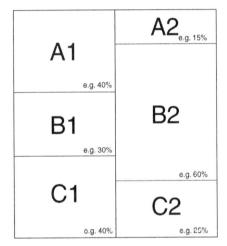

Alignment Score = 100 - K/2 where K = Abs(A1 - A2) + Abs(B1 - B2) + Abs(C1 - C2), Abs stands for absolute value, and A, B and C are percentages for comparable subgroups.

in half and subtracted from 100%. In the chart example, the score is 100 minus 60/2 or 70%. This score captures the alignment of all three characteristics in a single number. This number can be tracked as a baseline and turned towards 100% alignment.

This method can be used to compare three or more distributions. For example, if ABC is race/ethnicity and XYZ is gender, then the formula is adjusted by dividing K by four. The general rule is that K is divided by two times the number of groups adding to 100%.

It is important to understand that the alignment score can not be assessed in the same way that academic scores are evaluated. It is not necessarily true that alignment scores below 70% are "failing." Trend direction may be more important than absolute value.

APPENDIX M (See Chapter 3 Essay 27)

RBAing RBA in Anglicare Western Australia
(and Supplemental Implementation Research Measures)

Anglicare WA	
RBA on RBA: SELF-EVALUATION	
How Much?	**How Well?**
• # Staff • # Services/Programs • # of active services by phase • # of Staff involved in active services by phase	• Staff Satisfaction with training and support • #/ratio Trainers trained • Time it takes services to self-sustainability • Time programs spend in each stage • Validity of measures • Validity of data • % of programs implementing RBA
Is Anyone Better Off?	
• % of staff that understand what RBA is • % of staff that support RBA within Anglicare WA • % of staff that support RBA within their program at Anglicare WA • % of programs using RBA for program improvement • % of curves turned in right direction • % of programs with the capacity to use RBA unassisted	

Four Phases of Implementation

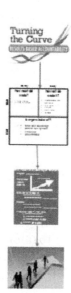

Turning the Curve

Phase 1 Awareness raising	• Emails • Presentations to groups
Phase 2 Service Planning	• Scoping and readiness assessment • Workshop • Define clients • Agree outcomes • Agree measures • Data strategy • Plot baselines
Phase 3 Service Implementation	• Data collection • Plot curves • Monitor and use
Phase 4 Normalise	• Refine • Use unassisted

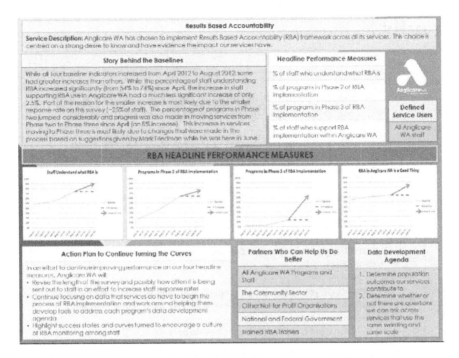

Supplemental RBA Implementation Research Questions and Measures
FPSI Draft 8/16/15

1. What is the extent of RBA implementation?

    % staff who attended RBA 101 and at least one Turn the Curve exercise

    % implementation score for the organization (as measured by the RBA SAQ)
        (or % of 18 SAQ items that are completed or in process)

    % of programs that have identified 3-5 headline measures using RBA methods

2. What is the effect of RBA implementation on performance?

    % of headline measures with a robust improvement strategy
        (developed using RBA methods)

    % of headline measures with a robust strategy that show a turned curve (at 6
        month intervals after strategy implementation)

3. Understanding and ease of use of RBA (stratified by training and program status)

    Rating (1-5) of staff who say they feel they understand RBA

    Rating (1-5) of staff who say they are using RBA and find it useful

    Rating (1-5) of staff who say RBA is easier to use than other methods (specify)

    % of staff who can give a reasonable explanation of the difference between
        population and performance accountability

    % of staff who can give a reasonable explanation of the "Turn the Curve"
        thinking process

4. What is the effect of RBA on organizational culture

    Rating (1-5) of staff who say RBA has helped clarify the purpose of their work

    Rating (1-5) of staff who say RBA has made communication within the
        organization easier

    Rating (1-5) of staff who say RBA opened the organization to more effective
        work with internal and external partners

Appendix N (See Chapter 5 Essay 7)

RBA/OBA Least Harm Cutback Exercise 1: POPULATION
Least harm to POPULATION quality of life (Population Accountability)

1. Identify a population result/outcome to which your organization most directly contributes. (e.g. Healthy People, Sustainable Environment, Children Ready for School)

2. What is your organization's role in contributing to this result/outcome?

3. What do you do that causes the greatest contribution?

4. What do you do that causes the least contribution? (Least harm cut candidates)

5. How could you change the way you do your work so as to make the same, or close to the same, contribution with less resources? (Least harm cut candidates)

> - Time: 5 minutes for each question
> - Record answers for each question.
> - Report 3 best ideas and reasoning

RBA/OBA Least Harm Cutback Exercise 2: PERFORMANCE
Least harm to CUSTOMERS' quality of life (Performance Accountability)

1. Identify one service.

2. Identify the primary customer group.

3. What are you doing that is most effective in improving the lives of your customers?

4. What is least effective? (Least harm cut candidates)

5. How could you change the way you do your work so as to make the same, or close to the same, contribution with less resources? (Least harm cut candidates)

> - Time: 5 minutes for each question
> - Record answers for each question.
> - Report 3 best ideas and reasoning

Appendix O (See Chapter 5 Essay 8)

FPSI FISCAL POLICY STUDIES INSTITUTE

7 Avenida Vista Grande #140 Santa Fe NM 87508

SOCIAL INVESTMENT BONDS (SIB) AND THE CHALLENGES OF SOCIAL INVESTING

Mark Friedman

The principle questions to be answered in social investing in general and Social Investment Bonds in particular are 1) What makes you think the investment will work? 2) How will the savings be calculated? 3) How will the savings be collected and distributed? and 4) How will you guard against perverse incentives and unintended consequences?

1) **What makes you think the investment will work?** From the work of Lisbeth Schorr and many others, we are practically drowning in good (often proven) ideas for social investment. These become the most promising bases for investment. Whatever approach you decide to take, make sure it is based on some tested ideas before going to scale.

2) **How will the savings be calculated?** Most prevention programs work in such a way that the expenditures are in one part of the budget and the savings are in another part of the budget, or in the budgets of other organizations, other levels of government or in other parts of society. There are countless examples. Health programs save the schools money. School programs save the criminal justice system money. Local child abuse prevention saves the national government money. Creating a methodologically sound way of calculating savings becomes progressively more difficult the greater the budget distance is between the investment and the return. In addition, social investment savings are almost always spread out over many years. Research has shown, for example, that investments in quality early childhood education produces savings in the criminal justice system 20 years later. How far into the future are investment savings to be calculated? Add to this the fact that most if not all such calculations are based on estimates, not fixed traditional accounting methods, and it quickly becomes clear that these estimates can vary widely in accuracy and credibility.

3) **How are the savings collected and distributed?** Even when you can credibly iden-

141

tify savings, just try to get the agency with the savings to hand over the cash. This almost always requires a set of written agreements that must be fully executed BEFORE the investment begins. Agreements between different levels of government or between the public and private sector are particularly difficult to engineer. If savings can be identified and collected, then who gets to keep them? Obviously, the first use of savings should be to repay the cost of the investment. That's the easy part. What happens to the "profit amount" is where the plot thickens. Does the money go to improve services, to reduce the budget deficit or to the coffers of a private corporation? Or are the profits split between the parties and if so, how? Anyone proposing that the profits of social investment go to private corporations is playing with fire. Why should we give money to corporations if we could finance the whole deal inside government (as has often been done)? How much is it FAIR for the corporation to keep? In some cases the profits have been embarrassingly large or otherwise difficult to defend and the payments to private companies can easily become a political embarrassment. For more information on this, see the FPSI 1994 paper: "The Pros and Mostly Cons of Contingency Fee Contracting for Revenue Enhancement Projects" And the 2007 paper "What You Need to Know About Privatization." both on the FPSI website publications page.

4) **How will you guard against perverse incentives and unintended consequences?** The prospect of private profit is what creates most of the problems here, but almost any financial reward scheme will be problematic. I was called in to clean up a deal like this that was so poorly written I had to terminate the contractor and reestablish the operation as a government run program. The original contractor then turned around and sued the state for $30 million dollars. After many thousands of dollars in state legal fees they finally settled for something like a million dollars. In almost every one of these deals, there will be places where decisions must be made (accept or don't accept a low skills person into a job training program, release or don't release a medium risk prisoner in a program to reduce recidivism, provide or don't provide expensive preventive treatment that might save later health costs) where private profit can be increased at the risk of public safety, health or some other public good. It is extremely difficult to anticipate every possible scenario and the ones you don't think about in advance are the ones that end up in court. When private profit is involved, the opportunities for mischief are almost endless. The fact that the SIB investment agent might be a nonprofit organization mitigates this problem, but only slightly. Everyone involved in the project from the manager on down will be under subtle if not explicit pressure to produce savings. As one of many examples, Missouri back in the 1990's provided financial incentives for social workers to return abused children back to their natural families in order to save foster care costs. It took only 3 weeks for people to wake up and see the risk to the safety of the children.

The idea that the profit motive can drive improvements in public services is very seductive. In truth, the private sector has a much overrated reputation for good management as evidenced by disasters in the oil and banking industries. Profit is fourth on the list of things that motivate people. Most people in the public sector will do the right thing for the right reasons without a profit motive. And, no matter what anyone says, running a government program is **more** complicated than running a business.

Bottom line: Swim at your own risk. No lifeguard on duty.

Draft #4: September, 2012

Appendix P (See Chapter 5 Essay 10)

A Q&A SESSION with WALES
(Thanks to Matt Jenkins and Adrian Davies)

Q: Is understanding of RBA principles more important than rigid fidelity to the RBA process?

> A: RBA is specifically designed so that it can be broadly and flexibly applied. I would always argue for understanding principles over rigid fidelity to RBA or any other model. Having said that, there are well thought out reasons for the conventions offered in RBA. For example, the difference between Population and Performance Accountability reflects real differences in the nature of efforts to improve quality of life as opposed to delivering services. It is not a distinction you could set aside and still say you were using RBA. Other parts of RBA, such as the Population and Performance talk to action 7 questions are central to the thinking process of RBA/OBA, and are best preserved in their original form, with commentary or supplemental material shown in parentheses. Most other material can be supplemented, adjusted, reordered or rephrased as circumstances dictate. A famous music teacher was once quoted as saying that you should learn the rules of harmony so you can decide when not to use them.

Q. Are sub-populations okay? How many layers can you have between services at the bottom and high level population outcomes? Does it matter?

> A. See the discussions of subpopulations at the beginning of Chapter 3 of *Trying Hard Is Not Good Enough*. One of the principle distinctions between Population Accountability and Performance Accountability is the service/customer relationship at the heart of all matters related to performance. Any time a group is defined in terms of its receipt of a particular service, it is a customer population and therefore part of Performance Accountability.
>
> Within Performance Accountability, there are higher/lower or larger/smaller customer populations. For example, the customer population of a particular service is smaller than the customer population of the whole agency which is smaller than the customer population of the service system to which the agency "belongs."
>
> In Population Accountability, populations and subpopulations can be defined in almost any way you like. In every case this definition must involve a geographic area. So for example, we could consider the well-being of the population

of all people in Wales, all children in Wales, all children in Cardiff, all children 0 to 5 in Cardiff, etc. RBA can be used for whole populations or subpopulations.

One place where subpopulation considerations are also important in RBA is in the "Story behind the baseline." If we are trying to understand the rate of teenage pregnancy, or school failure, it may be useful to examine how these problems are concentrated in certain areas or certain subpopulations so that we can tailor our efforts to greatest effect.

Another interesting part of the population / subpopulation discussion is the fact that "target populations" are part of Population Accountability. They represent the potential group from which actual customers are drawn, who then become part of the customer population.

The conclusion from all this is that there are not strict rules about how many levels there are in Population and Performance Accountability. It's as many levels as are needed.

Q: Can we have a hierarchy of outcomes? [e.g. by sub-population]

A: There is a long history to the confusion about "outcomes." The first matter of confusion has to do with language itself. What is meant by an "outcome" or a "result." I believe that the language discipline in RBA provides a template for how to reach agreement on a common language. In it's most basic form, you only need agreement on how to label ten ideas in order for people across government and the voluntary sector to talk to each other in a disciplined way. Those ten ideas are presented in the first section of the Tool for Choosing a Common Language (Appendix E)

Having said that, you can use RBA as a diagnostic tool to see if people have gotten ideas and words mixed up. It is not uncommon for the word "outcome" to be attached to several different ideas. Or for a single idea to have several different words associated with it. For example, in some of the original work on Every Child Matters (ECM) in England, they used a two tier outcome structure at the population level, but they called the two levels of outcomes by different names ("outcomes" and "aims"). When you look at the content of these two differently named things it turns out they are all quality of life statements and therefore they are all population "results" or "outcomes." In this case, ECM was proposing a two tier result or outcome structure at the top. Two and sometimes even three tier systems are not uncommon. But in TH pp. 53-54 you can see how it is often possible to simplify the structure by changing the third tier into indicators. It is likely that the sorting out you are thinking about has to do with first making clear the distinction between Population and Performance Accountability and then finding a disciplined way of using language to label important ideas like those ten discussed above.

Q. What similarities and differences are there between performance frameworks (generally) and RBA accountability?

A. This is a complex question, but here is a simple answer. Most other frameworks (1) do not clearly distinguish between Population and Performance Accountability, (2) often have a large and confusing set of performance measurement categories, in contrast to the three plain English ones used in RBA (*How much did we do? How well did we do it? Is anyone better off?*), and (3) many other frameworks are unwieldy, paper-intensive processes that are not actually useful to the people who have to fill out the forms, in contrast to the RBA 7 talk to action questions and simplified reporting formats

All people who have invented these kind of frameworks, including me, are essentially trying to do the same thing, that is provide tools to help make the world better. So comparing frameworks is a matter of judging which of these approaches works best for you. You might want to look at the end of TH Chapter 7 where I discuss "Comparing Frameworks," and suggest that you judge alternatives by how well they measure up against some simple criteria: "simple, common sense, plain language, minimum paper and useful."

There are, of course, other differences between RBA and traditional frameworks, including the use of baselines to judge progress, the use of targets only when they are fair and useful, and the emphasis on *no-cost/low-cost* ideas. But let me leave it at that for now.

Q. How credible is use of self-reporting tools on soft outcomes against more scientific tools?

A. This is a question about the reliability of data. There are basically two ways to know something in the social sciences. You can observe it (e.g. a person got a job or didn't, was re-admitted to hospital within 30 days or wasn't) or you can get some form of opinion from the customer, worker or third party. (e.g. the young person thought the mentoring program helped him or her do better in school, the older person thought the in-home attendant was kind, caring and helpful, the teacher thought the child was making progress on social skills, the parent reported better relations with his or her child etc.) We sometimes refer to reported opinion as "soft" data. And there are known problems associated with interpreting customer satisfaction data. But this does not mean that it is not important or does not have a place. My recommendation is always to use "soft" data in combination with data based on observable facts.

Q. How do you Turn the Curve when there is a lack of available data, or data takes time to come through? What do you do in the meantime?

A. This answer may sound a little odd. But imagine the most important measure you could conceivably have. Now you have two choices. You can create a "pseudo-baseline" as we do in the Turn the Curve exercise, where we estimate (1) where we are now on this measure, (2) what we think the history has been. Has it been getting better or worse or about the same?, and (3) where do we think it's headed in the future if we don't do something more or different than what we're doing now. This working version of a baseline can be used to drive the RBA Turn the Curve thinking process: What is the story behind the baseline? Who are the partners with a role to play in doing better? *What works* to do better? and What do we propose to actually do?

If for some reason you don't want to create a pseudo or working baseline, then you can simply reach a consensus on whether things are getting better or worse. In this case the direction of the baseline is used to drive the Turn the Curve discussion. This will feel unsatisfactory and will create a demand for the real data. And that may help you overcome the practical and political challenges of getting new data. But the process can still produce usable actions that will contribute to improvement.

The most extreme alternative would be to set aside data altogether and ask What is the purpose of the service? How are we doing and why? Who are the partners who could help? *What works*? Action Plan! If this progression helps, then use it. But this should make you curious about how to know the answer to the "How are we doing?" question. This inevitably requires some form of data. So create a Data Development Agenda and begin gathering the data you need to manage and improve the service. Workers in the organization will generally be more agreeable about gathering data if they can see from the beginning that it is needed to answer a fundamental question about the effectiveness of their work. Be careful not to gather more data than you need. Many data systems place unnecessary burdens on workers and actually detract from service delivery. Data systems should be useful to the line workers who generate the data. You might want to look into case management software, available from a number of different providers.

The principle here is NOT to wait for data or any other precondition to get started. Get started with what you have. Make informed guesses about what you don't have. Be deliberate about making the process better and more complete over time.

July 2010

Appendix Q (See Chapter 6 Essay 4)

THE RESULTS SCORECARD EXAMPLES
(Without the beautiful colors from the originals)

Children's Integrated Services Scorecard

CIS Scorecard

Population Accountability (to which our work contributes)

R Pregnant Women and Young Children Thrive	Time Period	Actual Value	Current Trend
I Percentage of Premature Births	2013	11.3%	↗ 1
I Percentage of Women Enrolled in WIC who Smoked During Pregnancy (last trimester)	2011	22.2%	↘ 1
I Percentage of Women who Received Early Prenatal Care (first trimester)	2012	79.4%	→ 2

R Children are Ready for School	Time Period	Actual Value	Current Trend
I Percentage of Children Ready for School According to the Vermont Kindergarten Readiness Survey	2013	49%	↘ 1

R Children Live in Stable, Supported Families	Time Period	Actual Value	Current Trend
I Number of Substantiated Child Abuse and Neglect Cases	2013	30	↘ 4

Program Performance Accountability (Our Performance)

P Children's Integrated Services	Time Period	Actual Value	Current Trend
PM How Much Number of Customers Served	FY 2015 Half 2	860	↗ 1
PM How Well Percentage of Referrals Triaged by CIS Coordinator	FY 2015 Half 2	90%	↘ 1
PM How Well Percentage of Participants with One or More Goal Met by Annual Review or Exit from Program	FY 2015 Half 2	84%	↗ 1
PM How Well Percentage of Participants with Two or Fewer CIS Service Professionals Interacting with the Family	FY 2014 Half 2	92%	↘ 1
PM How Well Percentage of Participants with a 6 Month Review Completed (from date of completed One Plan)	FY 2015 Half 2	71%	↗ 1
PM How Well Percentage of Participants with an Annual Review Completed (from date of completed One Plan)	FY 2015 Half 2	73%	↘ 1
PM How Well Percentage of Participants with a One Plan Meeting within 45 Days of Referral	FY 2015 Half 2	90%	↗ 2
PM How Well Percentage of Participants who had Services Start within 30 Days from Completed One Plan	FY 2015 Half 2	98%	↘ 1
PM Better Off Percent of Participants who Received a Screening/Assessment Within Required Time Line (45 days)	FY 2015 Half 2	86%	↘ 1
PM Better Off Percentage of Participants with no Further Need for Immediate Supports Upon Program Exit	FY 2015 Half 2	58%	↗ 1

Story Behind the Curve

Despite the gains over the past 5 years, more needs to be done to make sure the remaining 14% of adults are making healthier choices.

Factors that have contributed to improvement:

- Access to after school programs for students in our county
- Increased number of free smoking cessation programs
- Increased public awareness of threats to long term health

Limiting factors:

- Hard to tack the physical addiction of nicotine.
- Challenge of patients finding healthy ways to manage an increasing stress load

Based on the BRFSS question: "Do you now smoke cigarettes every day, some days, or not at all?" Persons are considered smokers if they reported smoking every day or some days.

Estimates based on fewer than 50 cases or with a confidence interval half-width of 10% or more ((upper CI-lower CI/100) >10) are considered unreliable and are not displayed.

Partners

- Doctors
- Smoking Cessation Programs
- Chamber of Commerce

What Works

Strategy

Appendix R (See Chapter 3 Essay 7)

BUSINESS   FINANCE   HEADLINES   HEALTH   TECHNOLOGY   WORLD   Search

Home / Business / New Zealand Government Chooses Results Scorecard™ Software to Manage Streamlined Contracting with NGOs

New Zealand Government Chooses Results Scorecard™ Software to Manage Streamlined Contracting with NGO

New Zealand's Ministry of Business, Innovation, and Employment will begin using the Results Scorecard™ performance and accountability software (developed by Results Leadership Group) to streamline and improve the contracting process between government and NGO partners.

Wellington, New Zealand (PRWEB) June 29, 2015

Results Leadership Group, developers of the Results Scorecard™ performance and accountability software, and New Zealand's Ministry of Business, Innovation, and Employment (MBIE) have just finalized a contract to have the Results Scorecard software support MBIE's Streamlined Contracting project. Over the next year, MBIE will begin rolling out the software to various ministries within New Zealand to manage and improve contracting processes between the government and NGO partners.

MBIE's Streamlined Contracting project aims to create greater consistency across government agencies, through the use of shared performance measures across programs to streamline reporting. This will reduce duplication and enable NGOs to focus on service delivery. MBIE has chosen the Results Scorecard to support these initiatives since the software offers an interactive interface to easily collaborate, share data, report on shared performance measures, manage projects and strategy, and improve community impact all in one integrated software tool.

Results Scorecard also uses and is built upon the Results-Based Accountability™ (RBA) framework-a decision-making framework used around the world to improve the lives of children, families, adults, and communities. In New Zealand, RBA is used across a wide range of sectors including social services, health and disability, local government, Whanau Ora, community development, environmental development, sports and recreation, and commercial sectors. RBA is incorporated within the Contracting Streamlining Framework as the mechanism to support an increased focus on outcomes in New Zealand's government contracting.

One of the hallmark features of RBA is the 'Turn the Curve' thinking process-a series of questions asked to help reverse a negative trend or accelerate a positive one within a community or organization. Results Scorecard's Turn the Curve Feature takes users through this process step-by-step, allowing them to focus on improving the most important measures and spending more time focusing on creating positive, measurable impact within the community.

Results Scorecard was chosen as the support tool for New Zealand's Streamlined Contracting project because it will allow MBIE to be more efficient and work in a more collaborative, coordinated, and disciplined way. With Results Scorecard it can spend more time focusing on making a difference and "Turning the Curve" on important measures, rather than figuring out how to report and share data.

To learn more about New Zealand MBIE's Streamlined contracting project and how they are using Results-Based Accountability, please visit http://www.business.govt.nz/procurement/procurement-reform/streamlined-contracting-with-ngos

To learn more about the Results Scorecard, please visit http://www.resultsscorecard.com

For the original version on PRWeb visit: http://www.prweb.com/releases/2015/06/prweb12809382.htm

Appendix S

Selected Readings and Resources

This is the updated section from the 10th Anniversary edition of TH. So much information is available on the web that you have to wonder if a book like this is even necessary. The rationale is that the material is scattered. Some would be hard to find. And collections make it more likely that some things will actually be read and used. The following section provides a lot more stuff you can access directly from the web.

BOOKS:

Chaos: Making a New Science, James Gleick, Penguin Books, 1987

Within Our Reach: Breaking the Cycle of Disadvantage, Lisbeth Schorr, Doubleday, 1988.

Complexity: The Emerging Science at the Edge of Order and Chaos, M. Mitchell Waldrop, Simon and Schuster, 1992.

Out of Control: The New Biology of Machines, Social Systems and the Economic World,Kevin Kelly, Perseus Books, 1994.

The Universe and the Teacup: The Mathematics of Truth and Beauty, K.C. Cole, Harcourt Brace and & Company, 1997.

Common Purpose: Strengthening Families and Neighborhoods to Rebuild America, Lisbeth Schorr, Doubleday, 1997.

The Tipping Point: How Little Things Can Make a Big Difference, Malcolm Gladwell, Back Bay Books, Little Brown and Co., 2000.

Poor Economics: A Radical Rethinking of the Way to Fight Global Poverty, Public Affairs, Abhijit Banerjee, Esther Duflo, 2012

Results Based Facilitation: Moving From Talk to Action, (Vols: Introduction, Foundation Skills, Advanced Skills), Sherbrooke Consulting Inc., Jolie Bain Pillsbury, 2013.

The Holy Grail of Public Leadership: And the Never-Ending Quest for Measurable Impact, Fourth Quadrant Publishing, Adam Luecking, 2013.

Who Is Driving The Bus: One Legislator's Road to Accountability, Fourth Quadrant Publishing, Diana S. Urban, 2014.

Stop Spinning Your Wheels: Using RBA to Steer Your Agency To Success, Fourth Quadrant Publishing, Anne McIntyre-Lahner, 2015.

Turning Curves: An Accountability Companion Reader, Mark Friedman, PARSE, 2015.

PAPERS:

The Cosmology of Financing: Financing Reform of Family and Children's Services: An Approach to the Systematic Consideration of Financing Options, Mark Friedman, The Center for the Study of Social Policy, 1994.

From Outcomes to Budgets: An Approach to Outcomes Based Budgeting for Family and Children's Services, Center for the Study of Social Policy, Mark Friedman, 1995.

The Future of Our Children: Long-term Outcomes of Early Childhood Programs, Center for the Future of Children, The David and Lucile Packard Foundation, Volume 5, Number 3, futureofchildren.org, Winter, 1995.

A Strategy Map for Results-based Budgeting: Moving from Theory to Practice, Mark Friedman, The Finance Project, September, 1996.

A Guide to Selecting Results and Indicators, Atelia I. Melaville, The Finance Project, May, 1997.

A Guide to Developing and Using Performance Measures in Results-Based Budgeting, Mark Friedman, The Finance Project, 1997.

A Guide to Developing and Using Family and Children's Budgets, Mark Friedman and Anna Danegger, The Finance Project, 1998.

Capturing Cash for Kids: A Workbook for Reinvesting in Community Based Prevention Approaches for Children and Families, The Comprehensive Integrated Services Reinvestment Project, Marty Giffin, Abram Rosenblatt, Nancy Mills and Mark Friedman, The Foundation Consortium for California's Children and Youth, 1998.

New Approaches to Evaluating Community Initiatives, Edited by Karen Fulbright-Anderson, Anne C. Kubisch, and James P. Connell, The Aspen Institute, 1998.

Reforming Finance, Financing Reform for Family and Children's Services, What Works Policy Brief, The Foundation Consortium for California's Children and Youth, Mark Friedman, January, 2000.

Results-Based Grantmaking: An Approach to Decision Making for Foundations and Other Funders, Mark Friedman, Fiscal Policy Studies Institute, October, 2000.

Results-Based Accountability for Proposition 10 Commissions: A Planning Guide for Improving the Well-Being of Young Children and Their Families, Mark Friedman, The UCLA Center for Healthier Children, Families and Communities, March, 2000.

Getting to Results: Data-Driven Decision-Making for Children, Youth, Families and Communities, What Works Policy Brief, Jacqueline McCroskey, PhD, The Foundation Consortium for California's Children and Youth, 2000.

Toward An Economics of Prevention: Illustrations from Vermont's Experience, Cornelius D. Hogan and David A. Murphey, Finance Project, December, 2000.

Informed Consent: Advice for State and Local Leaders on Implementing Results-Based Decision-making, Sara Watson, Finance Project, 2000.

Improving Children's Lives: A Tool Kit for Positive Results, Susan Robison, National Conference of State Legislatures, 2001.

Evaluation Methodology, Harvard Family Research Project *Evaluation Exchange,* Volume XI, No. 2, Summer, 2005.

Working Together to Improve Results: Reviewing the Effectiveness of Community Decision-Making Entities, Phyllis Brunson and partners, Center for the Study of Social Policy, 2006.

Turning Curves, Achieving Results: A Report of the Annie E. Casey Foundation's Children and Family Fellowship, Molly McGrath, Craig Levine, Brenda Donald, Dennis Campa, Yolie Flores Aguilar, AECF, 2007.

Better Outcomes for Children and Young People - From Talk to Action: UK Department for Children, Schools and Families, David Utting principle author, Crown Copyright, 2008.

ResultStat™: Driving Better Government Decisions with Data, Mark Friedman, Phil Lee, Adam Luecking and Andrew Boyd, Results Leadership Group, 2009.

Cardiff: What Matters: 2010:2020 - The 10 Year Strategy, Consultation Draft, December 2010.

Evaluation of Results-Based Accountability, Chronic Conditions Management Demonstrators Evaluation Report, prepared for the NHS Wales by Opinion Research Services (ccmdemonstrators.com), May 2011.

Key Indicator Systems: Experiences of Other National and Subnational Systems Offer Insights for the United States, US Government Accountability Office, Principle author Bernice Steinhardt, 2011.

What's Wrong With Logic Models, NSW Local Community Services Association (LCSA), Occasional Paper No. 1, Phil Lee, 2011.

Expanding the Evidence Universe, Lisbeth Schorr and Frank Farrow, Center for the Study of Social Policy, 2011.

Thought Exercises on Accountability and Performance Measures at the National Heart,Lung and Blood Institute (NHLBI): An Invited Commentary for Circulation Research, *Circulation Research*, American Heart Association, Circ. Res. 2011:108;405-409, 2011.

Results-Based Accountability: The road to better results: Targeting Capacity Building and Philanthropic Partnerships, Annie E. Casey Foundation, Phyllis Rozansky

The Vermont Accountability Compact, Benchmarks for Better Vermont and the Vermont Accountability Group, bbvt.marlboro.edu/#!compact/c185r, 2012.

Outcomes Project - Final Evaluation Report, Social Services Improvement Agency (SSIA), CordisBright Consulting Agency, 2013, check on line for final version and publication date.

Outcomes Based Accountability in Leeds: 'What is it like to be a child or young person in Leeds... And how do we make it better,' 2013

Next Generation Contracting: A Contract Reform Agenda for Funders and Non-profits, Fiscal Policy Studies Institute, Mark Friedman, 2013.

The Collective Impact Toolkit, Results Leadership Group, Justin Miklas, 2013.

Achieving Collective Impact with Results-Based Accountability, Results Leadership Group, Deitre Epps 2013.

Measuring Results in the Real World: A better way to link policy analysis and performance management: Mark Funkhouser, *Governing Magazine*, March, 2014.

Ten changes to reinvigorate children's social work, The Guardian, Andy Gill, 2014

A Community Partnership Planning Resource, The Government of South Australia, Department for Education and Child Development, www.decd.sa.gov.au/cpp/files/links/cppr_2014_v8.pdf, 2014.

An Evidence Framework to Improve Results, Lisbeth Schorr, Frank Farrow, Joshua Sparrow, Center for the Study of Social Policy, 2014.

Outcomes Based Accountability (in) Essex County Council, Strategy and Communications, Chelmsford, Essex, UK, 2014.

Collective Impact Using RBA, Fiscal Policy Studies Institute, Mark Friedman, 2014.

New Ways of Using Data in Federal Place-Based Initiatives: Opportunities to Create a Results Framework and Raise the Visibility of Equity Issues, Victor Rubin & Michael McAfee, whatcountsforamerica.org, 2014.

The Four Components of Effective Collective Impact: Through the Lens of Asset-Based Community Development and Results-Based Accountability™, Dan Duncan, Results Leadership Group, Asset-Based Community Development Institute, available resultsleadership.org, 2015.

Evaluation of Core Assets Support Programme: Using an Outcomes-Based Approach Making a difference to the life of Merthyr Tydfil's children and young people, Merthyr Tydfil Borough Council, (including contributions from Core Assets and Rob Hutchinson), March 2015 (search on line for final report).

How to Achieve the Performance Imperative with Results-Based Accountability, Results Leadership Group, Adam Luecking 2015.

OTHER RESOURCES:

Results-Based Accountability 101 Powerpoint Presentation: The complete Powerpoint presentation used in the basic 3 hour workshop on Results-Based Accountability 101 can be downloaded for free from resultsaccountability.com/workshops/materials/. The 45 page handout material that goes with the workshop can also be printed from this site. Use these materials to create your own presentation on Results-Based Accountability for your partners or coworkers (If you do this, please make sure you provide attribution. See also the notes on page 158).

Training for Trainers and Coaches: The Fiscal Policy Studies Institute and the Results Leadership Group offer training for those who wish to learn how to teach and coach Results-Based Accountability. These classes are offered from time to time and enrollment is limited. Future class announcements are posted to the website resultsaccountability.com.

The Results Scorecard is a powerful decision-making support software developed by the Results Leadership Group in 2010. It is designed to help non-profits and government agencies implement the RBA framework and create measurable collective impact for organizations and communities. It does so by connecting stakeholders in a single, interactive network, providing rapid access to data, and creating visual dashboards that can be used to improve decision-making and accelerate the RBA Talk-to-Action process. The software uses a simple and intuitive design, and the language can be customized to support each organization's unique terminology. Individuals interested in trying the Results Scorecard can sign up for a free trial at www.resultsscorecard.com.

VIDEO:

Building a Results-Based Accountability Framework: Video of the July 19, 1999 California Teleconference Presentation for Prop 10 (First 5) Commissions, with an introduction by Rob Reiner, sponsored by the California Children and Families First (First 5) State Commission, The California Endowment and the Foundation Consortium for California's Children and Youth. Copies available from the Fiscal Policy Studies Institute.

Results-Based Accountability 101 DVD: Full RBA 101 presentation by Mark Friedman (2.5 hours)- available from the Results Leadership Group - ordering information at resultsleadership.org.

RBA 101 Presentation to the Ontario Local Immigration Partnerships (LIPs) Conference, Toronto, Canada, youtube.com/watch?v=OsKb9YRxgt4, 2012.

Common Good Vermont: Vermont Nonprofit Legislative Day 2013: Mark Friedman on Results-Based Accountability, cctv.org/tags/RBA.

Mark Friedman Discusses Results-Based Accountability™ on CNBC Africa, resultsleadership.org/mark-friedman-discusses-RBA-cnbc-africa, October, 2014.

Notices regarding the use of Results-Based Accountability™ (RBA) material:

The RBA framework is free for use by government and nonprofit/NGO organizations. Limited permission is granted to **government and non-profit** organizations to use excerpts from this book and materials from the raguide.org and resultsaccountability.com websites. Such organizations may copy, distribute and use this material, providing it is done with full attribution and in the interest of improving the well-being of children, adults, families and communities. Materials may not be used for profit-making purposes without the express written consent of the Fiscal Policy Studies Institute Inc. and the Commissioner of Baseball. For purposes of this notice, profit making organizations include non-profit organizations that provide, and charge fees for, consulting services. Licensing fees and other requirements for use of RBA materials by for-profit organizations can be found at resultsleadership.org/results-based-accountability-licensing. Where there is any conflict between this notice and the website provisions, the website provisions take precedence. Small for-profit organizations (as defined on the web page) are not subject to licensing fees. Such organizations may get formal permission for free use of RBA material by sending an email request to markatfpsi@gmail.com.

A note about use of the trademark symbol. The purpose of using the trademark symbol for Results-Based Accountability™ and Outcomes Based Accountability™ is to protect against those (thankfully) rare instances where these names are misused. It is not intended to compromise the free use of RBA by government and nonprofit/NGO organizations. As a general rule, the ™ symbol needs to be used only once in a document, after which the names may be used without the symbol. Where use of the symbol is likely to be misinterpreted as restricting the use of proprietary material, it may be omitted. Note that the acronyms RBA and OBA are not copyrighted and no trademark symbol should be used.

About the Author

Mark Friedman has over four decades of experience in public administration and public policy and the scars to prove it. After one year as a high school math teacher, he worked 19 years for the Maryland Department of Human Resources, including six years as the Department's Chief Financial Officer. After leaving state service he spent four years with the Center for the Study of Social Policy in Washington D.C., and then 20 years as founder of the Fiscal Policy Studies Institute. That's 44 years if you were counting. Mark has published a wide range of papers on Results-Based Accountability and other topics and has spoken extensively across the US and around the world. He lives with his wife Terry in Santa Fe, New Mexico, too far away from his much loved children, Megan, Julie, and Aaron, and grandchildren, Mikayla, Carson, Bolton, Taylor, Tashi, Zachary and Sonam.

Made in the USA
Las Vegas, NV
13 May 2021